I0521125

From Quill to Keyboard
1861-1865

Civil War America's Most Important Words
In Plain English

JACK FITZGERALD

An Understandable History Book

Published by PerfectBound Publishing, LLC

ISBN: 979-8-9999207-2-0

First Edition

Cover design by Barbara M. Bustard

Printed in the United States of America

Table of Contents

Preface

This book walks readers through the biggest events of the Civil War, showing the most important documents and speeches the way they were originally written. But, because people spoke and wrote differently back then, it's sometimes hard to understand for those of us who speak in the language of the twenty-first century.

Because of that, this book also offers translations of those documents and speeches into modern language, the way we talk now. Why do we need to understand things that happened over 100 years ago? It's important because the things that have happened throughout history bring us to where we are now. And often, history seems to repeat itself. The events of the mid-1800s are especially relevant today as we find, once again, deeply divided beliefs and opinions about how the country should be run and who should matter the most. Sometimes, a look into the past can help us make decisions for the future.

The purpose of this book is not to provide a comprehensive history of everything related to the Civil War, but rather to highlight the most significant events in modern language. This aims to make history more accessible by rewriting it in plain English. The hope is that when you read excerpts or finish this book, you will be able to say, "That's understandable."

This book is part of the Understandable History Series.

Introduction – How Did It Come to This?

When Abraham Lincoln was first elected President of the United States in 1860, trouble had already long been brewing. The Southern states, whose agricultural economy depended greatly on slavery, were at odds with the Northern states, which mostly declared slavery to be wrong and inhumane. The South called this hypocrisy. The North mostly didn't keep slaves, but Northern mills needed the products of slave labor, such as cotton, as much as the South.

As the tension built leading up to Lincoln's election, abolitionists (people opposed to slavery) led by John Brown tried to get the slaves to revolt in Harper's Ferry, West Virginia (then still part of Virginia). On October 16, 1859, Brown's team captured the federal armory to steal weapons and arm the slaves. The group included a few free Black men, but no slaves joined the revolt. Within a few days, the local militia and townspeople surrounded Brown and his men. On October 18, then-Colonel Robert E. Lee stormed the

A Revolutionary Decision: Create a Nation or Address Slavery?

When our nation was being born, slavery was a big point of contention, but not the only one. Another major issue was states' rights, meaning whether each state had the right to govern itself, or whether the Federal government should make the laws for all. To many, this is what would decide whether the United States were united or not. Both issues had been angrily debated since long before the Union even existed.

This deep disagreement among the colonies is why the Declaration of Independence does not specifically address slavery. A passage in the original draft condemning slavery had to be removed or the Declaration most likely would never have been signed, and the United States might never even have been started. The colonial delegates to the Continental Congress on both sides knew they had to agree to this compromise and leave the slavery question to be decided by another generation.

arsenal, captured Brown and killed several in his group, including two of his sons.

John Brown was tried for treason, murder, and inciting slave rebellion. He was convicted and hanged on December 2, 1859 and was immediately seen as a martyr in the North. Even though the raid failed, the already-nervous South feared slave uprisings even more.

Lincoln's election added more fuel to the fire. His first inaugural address, the speech he gave on March 4, 1861, when he took office, focused on these issues. The years that followed were violent and bloody as Americans killed Americans over who was right and who would decide the future.

Chapter 1: A New Nation or Two Nations?

The signing of the United States Constitution in 1787 did not resolve all the disagreements among the delegates to the Constitutional Convention, nor those of the country's citizens. Among the unresolved topics were slavery and states' rights, hotly debated and nearly preventing the formation of the United States of America.

Once the founding fathers – the name often given to the signers of the Declaration of Independence and those who played important roles during the Revolutionary War era – decided not to explicitly address those issues, a pathway to unity opened and allowed the main focus to be separation from the rule of the British monarchy.

But the issues didn't go away. By the 1820s, tensions were rising, and tempers were flaring. Ultimately, these bitter disagreements led to states withdrawing from the Union, known as secession, which began officially in 1860. War broke out over these very strong differences of opinion, and it became more and more apparent that values, way of life, and the economy in different parts of the country were attached to those opinions.

Secession didn't happen overnight. Major events occurred that fanned the flames of anger and stirred the pot of contention for many people, leading from annoyance to outrage to violence, and to the Civil War of the United States. Here is the timeline:

1820s–1850s: The Buildup

1820 — Missouri Compromise
Missouri entered the Union as a slave state and Maine as a free state; slavery was officially banned north of the 36°30' line in the

Louisiana Territory. This temporarily balanced the free and slave states.

1831 — Nat Turner's Rebellion
A violent slave uprising in Virginia led to harsher slave laws in the South and increased tensions over slavery.

1850 — Compromise of 1850
California was admitted to the Union as a free state.

1850 — Fugitive Slave Act
Required that escaped slaves be returned when captured, even if they were found in a free state. It included harsh penalties for slaves AND for those who helped them, angering the North.

1852 — Harriet Beecher Stowe publishes *Uncle Tom's Cabin*
This anti-slavery novel inflamed Northern public opinion against slavery.

1854 — Kansas-Nebraska Act
Allowed settlers to decide on slavery by popular vote; led to violent clashes in what came to be called "Bleeding Kansas."

1857 — Dred Scott v. Sandford (Supreme Court decision)
Ruled that African Americans were not citizens and Congress had no power to ban slavery in the territories. This angered the North and pleased the South.

1858 — Lincoln-Douglas Debates
Public debates between Abraham Lincoln and Senator Stephen Douglas garnered national attention, highlighting the divisions over the expansion of slavery.

1859–1860: The Breaking Point

Oct 16, 1859 — John Brown's Raid on Harpers Ferry
Abolitionist John Brown attacks a federal arsenal, hoping to start

a slave rebellion. He is captured and executed. The South sees it as proof that the North supported slave revolts.

Nov 6, 1860 — Abraham Lincoln elected President
Lincoln wins without carrying a single Southern state. Southerners fear he will abolish slavery, even though he promised only to stop its expansion.

1860–1865: The Bloodshed

Dec 20, 1860 — South Carolina secedes
Less than 8 weeks after Lincoln's election, South Carolina becomes the first state to leave the Union, declaring that slavery was threatened.

Jan–Feb 1861 — Six more states secede
Mississippi, Florida, Alabama, Georgia, Louisiana, and Texas leave the Union.

Feb 9, 1861 — Confederate States of America formed
Jefferson Davis was chosen as president.

Mar 4, 1861 — Lincoln's First Inaugural Address
Lincoln promises not to interfere with slavery where it already exists but vows to preserve the Union.

Apr 12, 1861 — Battle of Fort Sumter
Confederates fire on a Union fort in South Carolina, and the Union surrenders the fort. The Civil War begins.

Apr–May 1861 — Four more states secede
Virginia, Arkansas, Tennessee, and North Carolina join the Confederacy after the attack on Fort Sumter.

1861 to 1865 — The Civil War
For 4 years, battles raged, destroying property and lives.

Wrap Up

The secession of eleven Southern states created two rival governments on the same continent, each claiming to be legitimate. While Lincoln insisted that the Union was unbreakable and secession illegal, the new Confederate States of America declared themselves independent. For several months, the crisis remained tense but mostly non-violent. That changed in April 1861, when Confederate forces fired on Fort Sumter, a U.S. military post in South Carolina. The attack forced the Union to surrender the fort. Within days, both sides were preparing to fight. What began as a political dispute over slavery and states' rights now erupted into a full-scale civil war.

Chapter 2: Not MY President—Lincoln's First Inaugural Address

March 4, 1861

Abraham Lincoln, the Republican candidate running for President of the United States, was elected on November 6, 1860. He ran against three other candidates. Stephen A. Douglas, a Northern Democratic senator, supported states' rights, which would allow the slavery issue to be decided by each state. John C. Breckinridge, a Southern Democrat who was serving as Vice President under James Buchanan, supported slavery in existing and new areas. John Bell, a former senator from Tennessee who ran under the Constitutional Union Party, tried to avoid the slavery issue altogether and only addressed keeping the Union together. This was similar to Lincoln's stance, but Lincoln firmly opposed allowing slavery to expand. Bell agreed to compromise wherever needed.

Lincoln won a clear majority in the Electoral College, but only about 40% of the people's votes, and he did not win in any Southern state. This was enough for him to be elected since his opponents were split three ways. It also helped that Lincoln was known nationally and respected, at least in the North, for being clear and consistent on the slavery issue.

Lincoln was inaugurated on March 4, 1861. It was typical at the time for presidents to be inaugurated in March instead of January, as they are now. A March swearing-in gave time for everyone to hear the news, travel to Washington, D.C., and certify the election results.

By March, after Lincoln had travelled from his home in Springfield, Illinois, seven states had already seceded from the Union, meaning they declared themselves no longer part of the United States. In total, eleven states would secede over time.

Just a few months later, violence erupted.

Below is the speech President Lincoln gave just before taking the oath of office, written in modern language to make it more understandable to modern readers. When facing a very divided nation, this is what he said:

Abraham Lincoln's First Inaugural Address

ORIGINAL LANGUAGE	MODERN LANGUAGE
Fellow-Citizens of the United States:	Fellow Americans,
In compliance with a custom as old as the Government itself, I appear before you to address you briefly and to take in your presence the oath prescribed by the Constitution of the United States to be taken by the President "before he enters on the execution of his office."	Following our usual tradition, today I will speak briefly and take the Oath of Office required by the Constitution before officially becoming President.
I do not consider it necessary at present for me to discuss those matters of administration about which there is no special anxiety or excitement.	I don't think it's important right now to talk about government issues that aren't causing much concern or debate.
Apprehension seems to exist among the people of the Southern States that by the accession of a Republican Administration their property and their peace and personal security are to be endangered. There has never been any reasonable cause for such apprehension. Indeed, the most ample evidence to the contrary	People in the South seem to fear that with a Republican President, their property, peace, and safety are at risk. But there's no good reason for this fear. In fact, I've often said otherwise.

has all the while existed and been open to their inspection.

I have no purpose, directly or indirectly, to interfere with the institution of slavery in the States where it exists. I believe I have no lawful right to do so, and I have no inclination to do so.

I have no intention of changing anything regarding slavery in the states where free people already own slaves. I don't think it would be legal for me to do that, and I personally don't want to.

Those who nominated and elected me did so with full knowledge that I had made this and many similar declarations and had never recanted them...

The people who nominated and elected me knew that I had said things like this before and had never taken those statements back.

It is seventy-two years since the first inauguration of a President under our National Constitution. During that period fifteen different and greatly distinguished citizens have in succession administered the executive branch of the Government. They have conducted it through many perils, and generally with great success. Yet, with all this scope for precedent, I now enter upon the same task for the brief constitutional term of four years under great and peculiar difficulty.

It's been 72 years since the first President took office under our Constitution. In that time, 15 highly respected men have been President. They've faced many dangers and usually succeeded. Now, I take on the same role for the next four years, but under especially difficult and unusual circumstances.

A disruption of the Federal Union, heretofore only menaced, is now formidably attempted. I hold that in

The breakup of the United States, which before was only a threat, is now being seriously attempted. I believe based on contemplation of universal law and of the Constitution the Union of these States is perpetual.

Perpetuity is implied, if not expressed, in the fundamental law of all national governments. It is safe to assert that no government proper ever had a provision in its organic law for its own termination.

Continue to execute all the express provisions of our National Constitution, and the Union will endure forever—it being impossible to destroy it except by some action not provided for in the instrument itself.

Again, if the United States be not a government proper, but an association of States in the nature of contract merely, can it, as a contract, be peaceably unmade by less than all the parties who made it?

I hold that in contemplation of universal law and of the Constitution the Union of these States is perpetual. I shall take care, as the Constitution itself expressly enjoins me, that the laws of the Union be faithfully executed in all the States.

the Constitution and as a generally held principle, that the Union is meant to last forever.

The idea that a nation will last forever is assumed in the laws of all governments, even if it is not clearly stated. It's fair to say that no government has ever written rules for how to end itself.

As long as we keep following the Constitution, the Union will last forever, because it can't be destroyed unless we do something the Constitution doesn't allow.

And even if the U.S. were just a contract between states, could that contract be peacefully broken without the agreement of all the states involved in the contract?

I believe, under both the law and the Constitution, that the Union is permanent. And I will do my duty, as the Constitution requires, to make sure the laws are enforced in every state.

Doing this I deem to be only a simple duty on my part; and I shall perform it, so far as practicable, unless my rightful masters, the American people, shall withhold the requisite means or in some authoritative manner direct the contrary.

I trust this will not be regarded as a menace, but only as the declared purpose of the Union that it will constitutionally defend and maintain itself.

In doing this there needs to be no bloodshed or violence; and there shall be none unless it be forced upon the national authority.

The power confided to me will be used to hold, occupy, and possess the property and places belonging to the Government and to collect the duties and imposts; but beyond what may be necessary for these objects, there will be no invasion—no using of force against or among the people anywhere.

Where hostility to the United States in any interior locality shall be so great and so universal as to prevent competent resident citizens from holding the Federal offices, there will be no attempt

I see this as a basic part of my job, and I'll carry it out as best I can unless the American people, who are my true bosses, take away the tools I need or officially tell me to stop.

I hope no one sees this as a threat. It's simply the Union saying it will defend and preserve itself in a way that follows the Constitution.

This can be done without bloodshed or violence, and there won't be any unless someone forces the government to defend itself.

I will use the power I've been given to hold and protect government property and to collect taxes and tariffs. There will be no invasion – no use of force against the people.

If a place is so hostile to the U.S. that no local citizen can safely serve in a federal job, we won't try to force outsiders on them just to fill the positions. I will not push Northerners into Southern offices or vice versa.

to force obnoxious strangers among the people for that object.

While the strict legal right may exist of the Government to enforce the exercise of these offices, the attempt to do so would be so irritating and so nearly impracticable withal that I deem it better to forego for the time the uses of such offices.

Even though the government might legally have the right to enforce the duties of these offices, doing so would cause too much tension and likely wouldn't work, so I think it's better to temporarily go without them.

The mails, unless repelled, will continue to be furnished in all parts of the Union.

Unless someone actively stops it, mail service will continue throughout the Union.

So far as possible the people everywhere shall have that sense of perfect security which is most favorable to calm thought and reflection.

As much as possible, I want people everywhere to feel safe and secure, so they can think clearly and calmly.

The course here indicated will be followed unless current events and experience shall show a modification or change to be proper...

I will stick to this plan unless future events and experience shows that changes are needed.

In your hands, my dissatisfied fellow-countrymen, and not in mine, is the momentous issue of civil war. The Government will not assail you.

To my fellow citizens who are unhappy, you and not me will be responsible for civil war if it happens. The government will not attack you.

You have no oath registered in heaven to destroy the Government, while I shall have

You are not sworn by any higher power to destroy the government, but I have taken the most solemn one to "preserve, protect, and defend it."

I shall take care, then, to have the laws executed.

If it be said that you are enemies of the Government, I cannot deny it.

But whether I or those whom I shall call to my aid shall be strong enough to suppress this rebellion, is yet uncertain.

You can have no conflict without being yourselves the aggressors.

I am loath to close. We are not enemies, but friends. We must not be enemies.

Though passion may have strained, it must not break our bonds of affection.

The mystic chords of memory, stretching from every battlefield and patriot grave to every living heart and hearthstone all over this broad land, will yet swell the chorus of the Union, when again touched, as surely they will be, by the better angels of our nature.

---

the solemn oath to "preserve, protect, and defend" it.

Therefore, I will make sure the laws are enforced.

If you claim to be enemies of the government, then I guess you are.

But whether I will be strong enough to end this rebellion, even with the support of those I call on for help, is not yet known.

There will be no conflict unless you are the ones to begin it.

I hate to end this speech. We are not enemies, but friends. We must not become enemies.

Even though emotions have been intense, our bonds of love and friendship must not be broken.

Thinking back on the battlefields of the American Revolution and the graves of the patriots should inspire us to listen to our own better natures. We should see each other as countrymen, not enemies.

Wrap Up

Lincoln's First Inaugural Address was delivered at a time of deep national crisis. Seven states had already said they were no longer part of the United States, and the country stood at the edge of war. In this speech, Lincoln tried to reassure the South that he would not interfere with slavery where it already existed, while firmly stating that secession was illegal and the Union must be preserved. His words showed both his desire for peace and his determination to protect the nation. Within weeks, however, compromise gave way to conflict, and the Civil War began.

Chapter 3: We're Outta Here: Secession and the Formation of the Confederacy

In all, 11 states seceded from the Union. Considering that there were only 36 states at the time (counting West Virginia and Nevada, which joined during the Civil War), that means almost a third left the United States to become part of the Confederate States of America.

Some of the 11 states that separated themselves from the Union didn't do so until after the Battle of Fort Sumter, when the seven original Confederate states attacked a Union military location and won. Over the next 2 years, four more states joined the Confederacy.

Here is a chart showing who's who during the Civil War Era, shown in alphabetical order. (Secession dates are listed in parentheses.)

UNION AND BORDER STATES	CONFEDERATE STATES
California	Alabama (1/11/1861)
Connecticut	Arkansas (5/5/1861)
Delaware*	Florida (1/10/1861)
Illinois	Georgia (1/19/1861)
Indiana	Louisiana (1/26/1861)
Iowa	Mississippi (1/9/1961
Kansas	N. Carolina (5/6/1861)
Kentucky*	S. Carolina (12/20/1860)
Maine	Tennessee (6/8/1861)
Maryland*	Texas (2/1/1861)
Massachusetts	Virginia (4/17/1861)
Michigan	
Minnesota	
Missouri*	
Nevada	
New Hampshire	
New Jersey	
New York	

Ohio
Oregon
Pennsylvania
Rhode Island
Vermont
West Virginia*
Wisconsin

Border States were mostly moderate, slaveholding but divided within themselves, and loyal to the Union. Missouri and Kentucky had strong Confederate leanings and were recognized by the Confederate States of America. However, neither officially seceded from the Union. The

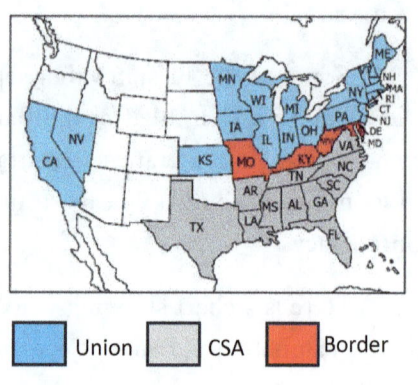

state of West Virginia was formed by splitting from Confederate Virginia over the issue of slavery.

States that officially seceded from the Union each wrote documents called Secession Ordinances. Virginia, Arkansas, North Carolina, and Tennessee wrote and adopted these ordinances following the attack by the Confederacy on Fort Sumter on April 12, 1861, which may have motivated their actions.

Secession Ordinance of Alabama

ORIGINAL LANGUAGE	MODERN LANGUAGE
An Ordinance to dissolve the union between the State of Alabama and the other States united under the compact styled "The Constitution of the United States of America"	This document dissolves Alabama's link to the Union and releases any obligation to be loyal to the Constitution of the United States of America.
Whereas, the election of Abraham Lincoln and Hannibal	Abraham Lincoln and Hannibal Hamlin, President and Vice

Hamlin to the offices of President and Vice-President … by a sectional party, avowedly hostile to the domestic institutions and to the peace and security of the people of the State of Alabama, preceded by many and dangerous infractions of the Constitution … by many of the States and people of the Northern section, is a political wrong of so insulting and menacing a character as to justify the people of the State of Alabama in the adoption of prompt and decided measures for their future peace and security, therefore:

President, were elected by the Republican party that only serves part of the nation and is openly hostile to Alabama's way of life. The Northern states repeatedly violate the U.S. Constitution by opposing slavery, refusing to uphold the Fugitive Slave Clause by not returning escaped slaves, and trying to take power away from individual states by claiming that secession is illegal. This threatens Alabama and insults its citizens, and justifies prompt action by Alabama's people to protect their own peace and security.

Section 1. Be it declared and ordained by the people of the State of Alabama, in Convention assembled, That the State of Alabama now withdraws, and is hereby withdrawn from the Union known as "the United States of America," … and henceforth ceases to be one of said United States, and is, and of right ought to be a Sovereign and Independent State.

Alabama's Convention officially declares that the state is leaving the United States and will no longer be a part of the Union. From now on, it exists as a fully independent state that makes and enforces its own laws.

Section 2. Be it further declared and ordained … That all powers over the Territory of said State, and over the people thereof, heretofore delegated to

All authority that was previously granted to the federal government over state territory and citizens is revoked. These powers are transferred back to the Government of the United States of America, be and they are hereby withdrawn from said Government, and are hereby resumed and vested in the people of the State of Alabama.

And as it is the desire and purpose of the people of Alabama ... to meet the slaveholding States of the South ... Be it resolved ... that the people of the States of Delaware, Maryland, Virginia, North Carolina, South Carolina, Florida, Georgia, Mississippi, Louisiana, Texas, Arkansas, Tennessee, Kentucky and Missouri ... are hereby invited to meet ... on the 4th day of February, A.D., 1861 ... at the city of Montgomery ... for the purpose of consulting ... for our common peace and security. And be it further resolved ... That the President of this Convention ... be instructed to transmit forthwith a copy of the foregoing Preamble, Ordinance, and Resolutions to the Governors of the several States named ... Done ... at Montgomery, on this, the eleventh day of January, A.D. 1861.

the people and government of Alabama.

Alabama invites all fellow slaveholding states to send delegates to a convention in Montgomery on February 4, 1861. The goal is to discuss forming a coordinated and permanent government to secure peace and safety. Invited states are Delaware, Maryland, Virginia, North Carolina, South Carolina, Florida, Georgia, Mississippi, Louisiana, Texas, Arkansas, Tennessee, Kentucky, and Missouri. The President of Alabama's Convention is instructed to immediately send them a copy of this ordinance and its resolutions.

This was formalized in Montgomery on January 11, 1861.

Secession Ordinance of Arkansas

ORIGINAL LANGUAGE	MODERN LANGUAGE
An Ordinance to dissolve the union now existing between the State of Arkansas and the other States united with her under the compact entitled "The Constitution of the United States of America"	A formal document to dissolve ties between Arkansas and the Union, and to withdraw from any requirements to obey "The Constitution of the United States of America"
Whereas, in addition to the well-founded causes of complaint set forth by this convention, in resolutions adopted on the 11th March, A.D. 1861, against the sectional party now in power in Washington City, headed by Abraham Lincoln, he has, in the face of resolutions passed by this convention pledging the State of Arkansas to resist to the last extremity any attempt on the part of such power to coerce any State that had seceded from the old Union, proclaimed to the world that war should be waged against such States, until they should be compelled to submit to their rule... and large forces ... are now being marshaled ... to carry out this inhuman design; and to longer submit to such rule ... would be disgraceful and ruinous to the State of Arkansas:	This ordinance declares that Arkansas is no longer part of the United States. This supports another document written by the Arkansas Convention on March 11, 1861. Arkansas criticizes President Lincoln's administration for promising to use force to subdue seceded states even though Arkansas had pledged to resist such coercion. Any continued submission is humiliating and destructive to Arkansas.

Therefore, we, the people of the State of Arkansas, in convention assembled, do hereby declare and ordain, ... that the "ordinance and acceptance of compact," passed and approved by the General Assembly ... on the 18th day of October, A.D. 1836 ... and all other laws ... whereby the State of Arkansas became a member of the Federal Union, be ... repealed, abrogated, and fully set aside; and the union now subsisting ... under the name of the United States of America, is hereby forever dissolved.

Thus, the people of Arkansas officially cancel the state's original constitution, laws, and compact that joined it to the United States in 1836. From now on, the membership of Arkansas in the United States is permanently ended.

And we do further hereby declare and ordain, That the State of Arkansas hereby resumes to herself all rights and powers heretofore delegated to the government of the United States ... that her citizens are absolved from all allegiance to said Government ... and that she is in full possession and exercise of all the rights and sovereignty which appertain to a free and independent State.

Arkansas now takes back all powers previously given to the federal government. Its citizens are released from loyalty to the U.S. and Arkansas stands fully independent, exercising all related rights.

We do further ordain and declare, That all rights acquired and vested under the Constitution of the United States ... or ... any act or acts of Congress, or treaty, or under any law of this State, and not

Any rights that Arkansas citizens were given under U.S. law, federal treaties, congressional acts, or state laws will continue unchanged as if secession had not occurred, so

incompatible with this ordinance, shall remain in full force and effect ... and have the same effect as if this ordinance had not been passed.	long as they don't conflict with this ordinance.
Adopted and passed in open convention on the 6th day of May, A.D. 1861.	This ordinance is officially adopted and ratified by the Arkansas Convention on May 6, 1861.

Secession Ordinance of Florida

ORIGINAL LANGUAGE	MODERN LANGUAGE
We, the people of the State of Florida, in Convention assembled, do solemnly ordain, publish and declare:	The Convention of the State of Florida officially declares:
That the State of Florida hereby withdraws herself from the confederacy of States existing under the name of the United States of America, and from the existing Government of said States; and that all political connection between her and the Government of said States ought to be and the same is hereby totally annulled, and said Union of States dissolved; and the State of Florida is hereby declared a Sovereign and Independent Nation; and that all ordinances heretofore adopted in so far as they create or recognize said Union, are rescinded; and all laws or parts of laws in force in this State, in	On January 10, 1861, Florida's people officially declare that Florida withdraws from the United States of America and completely rejects the federal government. Any political ties with the federal government are released and the Union between the states is ended. Florida is henceforth an independent nation. Any prior laws, ordinances, or statutes that recognized the federal Union are no longer in effect in Florida.

so far as they recognize or assent to said Union, are rescinded; and all laws or parts of laws in force in the State, in so far as they recognize or assent to said Union, be, and they are hereby repealed. Done in open Convention, January 10th, A. D.1861.

Secession Ordinance of Georgia

ORIGINAL LANGUAGE	MODERN LANGUAGE
An Ordinance to dissolve the Union between the State of Georgia and other States united with her under a compact of Government entitled "the Constitution of the United States of America."	Georgia officially declares that it is dissolving its membership in the union of states governed by the U.S. Constitution.
We, the people of the State of Georgia, in Convention assembled, do declare and ordain, and it is hereby declared and ordained: That the ordinance adopted by the people of the State of Georgia in Convention on the second day of January in the year of our Lord seventeen hundred and eighty-eight, whereby the Constitution of the United States of America was assented to, ratified and adopted; and also all acts and parts of acts of the General Assembly of this State ratifying and adopting amendments of	Georgia cancels the original ordinance from January 2, 1788, when it approved the U.S. Constitution, and all related laws and constitutional amendments passed by its legislature. Georgia now completely ends its legal commitment to the federal government.

the said Constitution, are hereby repealed, rescinded and abrogated.	
We do further declare and ordain, That the Union now subsisting between the State of Georgia and other States, under the name of the "United States of America," is hereby dissolved, and that the State of Georgia is in the full possession and exercise of all those rights of sovereignty which belong and appertain to a free and independent State. Passed January 19, 1861.	The existing union between Georgia and the other United States is officially ended. Georgia now fully possesses and exercises all rights of a free and independent nation-state. This ordinance is formally adopted in the Georgia Secession Convention on January 19, 1861.

Secession Ordinance of Louisiana

ORIGINAL LANGUAGE	MODERN LANGUAGE
An Ordinance to dissolve the union between the State of Louisiana and other States united with her under the compact entitled "The Constitution of the United States of America."	Louisiana formally declares it is ending its constitutional relationship with the United States under the U.S. Constitution.
We, the people of the State of Louisiana, in convention	Louisiana declares that its 1811 ordinance approving the U.S.

assembled, do declare and ordain, and it is hereby declared and ordained, That the ordinance passed by us in convention on the 22d day of November, in the year eighteen hundred and eleven, whereby the Constitution of the United States of America and the amendments of the said Constitution were adopted, and all laws and ordinances by which the State of Louisiana became a member of the Federal Union, be, and the same are hereby, repealed and abrogated; and that the union now subsisting between Louisiana and other States under the name of "The United States of America" is hereby dissolved.

We do further declare and ordain, That the State of Louisiana hereby resumes all rights and powers heretofore delegated to the Government of the United States of America; that her citizens are absolved from all allegiance to said Government; and that she is in full possession and exercise of all those rights of sovereignty which appertain to a free and independent State.

We do further declare and ordain, that all rights acquired

Constitution, as well as any other related laws and ordinances, are completely rejected. The existing Union between Louisiana and the United States is officially dissolved.

Louisiana formally takes back all powers previously given to the federal government. Its citizens are released from their obligation to be loyal to the United States, and Louisiana now fully exercises all rights of an independent nation.

Any rights previously granted under the U.S. Constitution,

and vested under the Constitution of the United States, or any act of Congress, or treaty, or under any law of this State, and not incompatible with this ordinance, shall remain in force and have the same effect as if this ordinance had not been passed.	federal laws, treaties, or existing Louisiana laws remain valid as if secession had not occurred unless they conflict with this ordinance.
Adopted in convention at Baton Rouge this 26th day of January, 1861.	Alabama officially adopted this ordinance on January 26, 1861, during the Secession Convention held in Baton Rouge.

Secession Ordinance of Mississippi

ORIGINAL LANGUAGE	MODERN LANGUAGE
An Ordinance to Dissolve the Union Between the State of Mississippi and Other States United with Her Under the Compact Entitled "The Constitution of the United States of America."	Mississippi Declares Independence from the United States
The people of the State of Mississippi, in Convention assembled, do ordain and declare, and it is hereby ordained and declared as follows, to-wit:	The people of Mississippi held a formal meeting at which they adopted this ordinance to end membership in the Union.
Section 1st. That all the laws and ordinances by which the said State of Mississippi became a member of the Federal Union of the United States of America be, and the same are hereby	Mississippi cancels all laws and agreements it approved when it joined the U.S. It formally withdraws all requirements to follow those federal laws. The state now takes back all

repealed, and that all obligations on the part of the said State or the people thereof to observe the same, be withdrawn, and that the said State doth hereby resume all the rights, functions and powers which... were conveyed to the government of the said United States, and is absolved from all the obligations... incurred to the said Federal Union, and shall... henceforth be a free, sovereign and independent State.

authority previously given to the national government, is freed from anything required by the Constitution of the U.S. and declares itself an independent state that makes and enforces its own laws.

Section 2nd. That so much of the first section of the seventh article of the Constitution of this State as requires members of the Legislature, and all officers, executive and judicial, to take an oath or affirmation to support the Constitution of the United States, be, and the same is hereby abrogated and annulled.

Any part of Mississippi's constitution, specifically Article VII which mandates state officials (legislative, executive, or judicial) to swear allegiance to the U.S. Constitution, is no longer in effect. Those officials are no longer required to be loyal to the federal government.

Section 3rd. That all rights acquired and vested under the Constitution of the United States, or under any act of Congress... or under any law of this State, and not incompatible with this Ordinance, shall remain in force and have the same effect as if this Ordinance had not been passed.

Any rights previously granted under the U.S. Constitution, federal laws, treaties, or Mississippi law are still valid unless they conflict with this ordinance.

Section 4th. That the people of the State of Mississippi hereby

Mississippi will join in a new federal union composed of

consent to form a Federal Union with such of the States as may have seceded or may secede from the Union... upon the basis of the present Constitution of the said United States, except such parts thereof as embrace other portions than such seceding States.	states that have seceded or will secede from the United States and from following the existing U.S. Constitution, except for certain sections related to states did not secede. Mississippi joins in forming a confederation of seceded states under a new Constitution.
Thus ordained and declared in Convention the 9th day of January, in the Year... 1861. ... signed by the President and Members of this Convention this the fifteenth day of January, A. D., 1861.	This ordinance is formally adopted on January 9, 1861, at Mississippi's Secession Convention. It was signed by the president and delegates of the convention on January 15, 1861 to formalize their commitment.

Secession Ordinance of North Carolina

ORIGINAL LANGUAGE	MODERN LANGUAGE
An Ordinance to dissolve the union between the State of North Carolina and the other States united with her under the compact of government entitled "The Constitution of the United States."	North Carolina declares it is ending its membership in the United States, originally joined by approving the U.S. Constitution.
We, the people of the State of North Carolina in convention assembled, do declare and ordain, and it is hereby declared and ordained, That the ordinance adopted by the State of North Carolina in the convention of 1789, whereby the Constitution of the United	The convention declares that North Carolina's 1789 ordinance approving the U.S. Constitution is canceled and no longer valid. This also applies to any amendments to the Constitution.

ORIGINAL LANGUAGE	MODERN LANGUAGE
States was ratified and adopted, and also all acts and parts of acts of the General Assembly ratifying and adopting amendments to the said Constitution, are hereby repealed, rescinded, and abrogated.	
We do further declare and ordain, That the union now subsisting between the State of North Carolina and the other States under the title of the United States of America, is hereby dissolved, and that the State of North Carolina is in full possession and exercise of all those rights of sovereignty which belong and appertain to a free and independent State.	The convention decided that the Union between North Carolina and the United States is officially dissolved. From this point on, North Carolina holds and exercises all the powers and rights of an independent nation that makes and enforces its own laws.
Done in convention at the city of Raleigh, this the 20th day of May, in the year of our Lord 1861, and in the eighty-fifth year of the independence of said State.	This ordinance is passed in Raleigh on May 20, 1861, marking 85 years since North Carolina first declared independence from Great Britain in 1776.

Secession Ordinance of South Carolina

ORIGINAL LANGUAGE	MODERN LANGUAGE
An Ordinance to dissolve the union between the State of South Carolina and other States united with her under the compact entitled "The Constitution of the United States of America."	South Carolina formally declares it is ending its membership in the United States, which it had joined by signing the U.S. Constitution.

"We, the people of the State of South Carolina, in Convention assembled, do declare and ordain, and it is hereby declared and ordained, that the ordinance adopted by us in convention on the twenty-third day of May, in the year of our Lord one thousand seven hundred and eighty-eight, whereby the Constitution of the United States of America was ratified, and also all acts and parts of acts of the General Assembly of this State ratifying amendments of the said Constitution, are hereby repealed; and that the union now subsisting between South Carolina and other States, under the name of the 'United States of America,' is hereby dissolved."	South Carolina officially cancels the ordinance it approved in 1788 to follow the U.S. Constitution and its amendments. It also formally ends its membership in the United States.

Secession Ordinance of Tennessee

ORIGINAL LANGUAGE	MODERN LANGUAGE
Declaration of Independence and Ordinance dissolving the federal relations between the State of Tennessee and the United States of America."	Tennessee declares its independence from the United States and announces an official ending of its federal relationship with the Union.
First. We, the people of the State of Tennessee, waiving any expression of opinion as to the abstract doctrine of secession, but asserting the right, as a free	Tennessee claims the right to change its government and officially cancels all laws it agreed to when it entered the Union. It no longer has any

and independent people, to alter, reform, or abolish our form of government in such manner as we think proper, do ordain and declare that all the laws and ordinances by which the State of Tennessee became a member of the Federal Union of the United States of America are hereby abrogated and annulled, and that all the rights, functions and powers which by any of said laws and ordinances were conveyed to the Government of the United States, and to absolve ourselves from all the obligations, restraints, and duties incurred thereto; and do hereby henceforth become a free, sovereign, and independent State.

requirement to give any power to the U.S. government. From this moment forward, Tennessee exists as a fully independent state that makes and enforces its own laws.

Second. We furthermore declare and ordain that article 10, sections 1 and 2, of the constitution of the State of Tennessee, which requires members of the General Assembly and all officers, civil and military, to take an oath to support the Constitution of the United States be, and the same are hereby, abrogated and annulled, and all parts of the constitution of the State of Tennessee making citizenship of the United States a qualification for office and

Tennessee's state officials are no longer required to swear loyalty to the U.S. Constitution. U.S. citizenship is no longer required for holding a government job, and Tennessee's state employees do not need to recognize the U.S. Constitution.

recognizing the Constitution of the United States as the supreme law of this State are in like manner abrogated and annulled.	
Third. We furthermore ordain and declare that all rights acquired and vested under the Constitution of the United States, or under any act of Congress passed in pursuance thereof, or under any laws of this State, and not incompatible with this Ordinance, shall remain in force and have the same effect as if this Ordinance had not been passed.	Any rights granted under the U.S. Constitution remain unchanged as if secession had never occurred, so long as they do not conflict with this ordinance.
Ratified by popular vote—approval by 104,471 to 47,183 on June 8, 1861.	Tennessee's ordinance was put to a public vote and approved by a large majority on June 8, 1861, formally making it state law.

Secession Ordinance of Texas

ORIGINAL LANGUAGE	MODERN LANGUAGE
An Ordinance to dissolve the Union between the State of Texas and the other States united under the compact styled "The Constitution of the United States of America."	This document announces that relationship of Texas to the Union is dissolved, and separates Texas from the Constitution of the United States of America.
Whereas, the Federal Government has failed to accomplish the purposes of the	Texas states the government has failed in its duty to protect frontier citizens and property.

compact of union... in providing protection... to the persons of our people upon an exposed frontier, or to the property of our citizens; and, whereas, the action of the Northern States ... is violative of the compact ... and, whereas, the recent developments ... make it evident that the power of the Federal Government is sought to be made a weapon with which to strike down the interests ... of the people of Texas and her sister slaveholding States, instead of permitting it to be ... our shield against outrage and aggression: Therefore,

We, the People of the State of Texas, by Delegates in Convention assembled, do declare and ordain that the ordinance adopted by our convention ... on the Fourth day of July, A.D. 1845 ... under which the Republic of Texas was admitted into Union ... be, and is hereby, repealed and annulled; that all the powers which ... were delegated by Texas to the Federal Government, are revoked and resumed; that Texas is of right absolved from all restraints and obligations incurred by said compact, and is a separate sovereign State, and that her citizens and people are absolved from all allegiance to the United States, or the Government thereof.

Texas charges that Northern states are violating constitutional guarantees such as the right to own slaves and the right of states to make their own decisions. The federal government is being misused, and this harms Texas and other states that keep slaves.

Texas formally cancels its 1845 agreement to become part of the U.S. All powers that were given to the federal government are now taken back. Texas is now a separate, independent state that makes and enforces its own laws, and its people are not required to be loyal to the U.S. government.

ORIGINAL LANGUAGE	MODERN LANGUAGE
This ordinance shall be submitted to the people of Texas for their ratification or rejection by the qualified voters thereof, on the 23rd day of February 1861, and unless rejected by a majority of the votes cast, shall take effect and be in force on and after the 2nd day of March, A.D. 1861. Provided, that in the Representative District of El Paso, said election may be held on the 19th day of February, A.D. 1861.	This ordinance will be put before voters on February 23, 1861, (or February 19 in the El Paso district). If not rejected by a majority, it will go into effect on March 2, 1861.
Done by the People of the State of Texas, in Convention assembled, at Austin, this 1st day of February, A.D. 1861.	Officially adopted in Austin on February 1, 1861, by delegates to the Secession Convention.

Secession Ordinance of Virginia

ORIGINAL LANGUAGE	MODERN LANGUAGE
An Ordinance to repeal the ratification of the Constitution of the United States of America, by the State of Virginia, and to resume all the rights and powers granted under said Constitution.	Virginia formally takes back its approval of the U.S. Constitution and reclaims all powers it had previously granted to the federal government.
The people of Virginia, in their ratification of the Constitution of the United States of America, adopted by them in Convention on the twenty-fifth day of June, in the year of our Lord one thousand seven hundred and eighty-eight, having declared	In 1788, when Virginia approved the U.S. Constitution, it stated that the powers it was granting came from the people and could be taken back if the government abused them. Virginia now claims that the federal government has indeed

that the powers granted under said Constitution were derived from the people of the United States and might be resumed whensoever the same should be perverted to their injury and oppression, and the Federal Government having perverted said powers not only to the injury of the people of Virginia, but to the oppression of the Southern slave-holding States:

abused these powers, harming Virginians and not serving the interests of Southern states that own slaves.

Now, therefore, we, the people of Virginia, do declare and ordain, That the ordinance adopted by the people of this State in Convention on the twenty-fifth day of June, in the year of our Lord one thousand seven hundred and eighty-eight, whereby the Constitution of the United States of America was ratified, and all acts of the General Assembly of this State ratifying or adopting amendments to said Constitution, are hereby repealed and abrogated; that the union between the State of Virginia and the other States under the Constitution aforesaid is hereby dissolved, and that the State of Virginia is in the full possession and exercise of all the rights of sovereignty which belong and appertain to a free and independent State.

Therefore, Virginia takes back its 1788 approval of the U.S. Constitution and all related state laws adopting amendments. Virginia's union with the other states is dissolved, and Virginia now fully takes back and exercises all the rights of an independent state.

And they do further declare, that said Constitution of the United States of America is no longer binding on any of the citizens of this State.	Virginia further declares that the U.S. Constitution no longer has authority over any Virginian citizen.
This Ordinance shall take effect and be an act of this day, when ratified by a majority of the votes of the people of this State, cast at a poll to be taken thereon on the fourth Thursday in May next, in pursuance of a schedule hereafter to be enacted.	The ordinance will only take legal effect if approved by a majority of Virginians in a vote scheduled for the May 4, 1861.
Done in Convention in the city of Richmond, on the seventeenth day of April, in the year of our Lord one thousand eight hundred and sixty-one, and in the eighty-fifth year of the Commonwealth of Virginia.	This ordinance is adopted in Richmond on April 17, 1861, marking the 85th year since Virginia declared independence from Great Britain in 1776.

Wrap Up

Missouri and Kentucky are sometimes considered the twelfth and thirteenth Confederate states due to their strong dissatisfaction with the policies of the Union (Republican) government and the divided opinions of their citizens. While both states drafted secession documents, neither officially seceded. Some of Missouri's legislators drafted an Ordinance of Secession but then fled in 1861 after Union forces drove the official state government from Jefferson City. The ordinance was approved in exile by that pro-Confederate faction, but the statewide Missouri Constitutional Convention rejected secession.

Similarly, Kentucky pro-Confederate delegates created an Ordinance of Secession, but it was not supported nor enacted by the recognized state government.

Chapter 4: Birth of the Confederacy: Jefferson Davis's First Inaugural Address

February 18, 1861

No matter how we personally feel about states seceding from the Union, not everyone agreed on whether that was legal. The Confederate States of America claimed it legitimately existed as an independent nation from February 8, 1861 to May 5, 1865 but was never recognized by the United States.

Nevertheless, the South elected Jefferson Davis as its President. He took the oath of office on February 18, 1861, and delivered an inaugural speech, shown below in its original language and with a modern translation to make it easier for today's readers to understand.

Jefferson Davis's Inaugural Address

ORIGINAL LANGUAGE	MODERN LANGUAGE
Gentlemen of the Congress of the Confederate States of America, Friends, and Fellow-Citizens:	Members of Congress, friends, and fellow citizens:
Called to the difficult and responsible station of Chief Magistrate of the Confederate States, I approach the discharge of the duties assigned to me with an humble distrust of my own abilities, sustained by the hope that the same kindness which was extended to me in the less arduous position which I have heretofore occupied will be generously accorded to me now. I fully realize the weight of responsibility and the	I have been called to serve as President of the Confederate States, and I have to wonder if I am up to this enormous task. I hope you will continue to support me as President as you have supported me in the past. I know this is going to be hard but with your help and God's blessing, I believe we can build a strong new government.

magnitude of the task before me, but I trust that with your help and the blessing of God we shall succeed in establishing our new government on a firm foundation.

Our present political position has been achieved in a manner unprecedented in the history of nations. It illustrates the American idea that governments rest upon the consent of the governed, and that it is the right of the people to alter or abolish governments whenever they become destructive of the ends for which they were established. The declared purpose of the compact of union from which we have withdrawn was to "establish justice, insure domestic tranquility, provide for the common defense, promote the general welfare, and secure the blessings of liberty to ourselves and our posterity;" and when, in the judgment of the sovereign States composing this Confederacy, it had been perverted from the purposes for which it was ordained, and ceased to answer the ends for which it was established, a peaceful appeal to the ballot box declared that the government created by that compact should cease to exist.

Our forming a new nation is based on the belief that governments only exist with the agreement of the people who are governed, and those people have a right to change or end it if it no longer serves their purpose. The goals of the U.S. Constitution were to provide peace, justice, prosperity, and liberty, and to defend its citizens. The Confederacy believes it no longer meets these goals, so we peacefully voted to withdraw from participating in the Union. We are exercising our "inalienable rights" as stated in the Declaration of Independence of 1776. Each state decided for itself when to exercise that right.

In this we merely asserted the right which the Declaration of Independence of 1776 defined to be "inalienable." Of the time and occasion of its exercise, they, as sovereigns, were the final judges, each for itself.

The impartial and enlightened verdict of mankind will vindicate the rectitude of our conduct; and He who knows the hearts of men will judge of the sincerity with which we have labored to preserve the government of our fathers in its spirit. The right solemnly proclaimed at the birth of the United States, and which has been affirmed and reaffirmed in the bills of rights of States subsequently admitted into the Union of 1789, undeniably recognizes in the people the power to resume the authority delegated for the purposes of government. Thus the sovereign States here represented proceeded to form this Confederacy; and it is by abuse of language that their act has been denominated a revolution. They formed a new alliance, but within each State its government has remained, so that the rights of person and property have not been disturbed.

We think the world will agree with and support us when they know and understand our position. God knows we are sincere in keeping to the basic principles of the Declaration. We are reclaiming our political authority and that's why we are forming the Confederacy. We do not view our actions as a "revolution." Each state has been maintained as it was; people's rights have not been changed. We have simply created a new union.

It is indeed a new government, but the object is to secure for each State the rights which were theirs before the Union was formed. Our present condition, achieved in a manner so remarkable, cannot fail to challenge the respect of mankind; and I earnestly hope will be of service to cause the moral and physical well-being of the people to be maintained and improved.

If a just perception of political rights, and a determination to maintain them, have suggested the measure of separation, we have reason to be assured that our Constitution, framed by the same wisdom, and guarded by the same watchfulness, will be administered in the spirit of justice, and will ensure to every citizen the full enjoyment of the rights it was intended to secure, and will perpetuate our government; and, if so, it will be the best guarantee of permanent peace with our former associates.

But if we are mistaken in the ability of our people to govern themselves, and if they are unfit for self-government, the

This might be a new government, but the rights each state already had will be protected under our new Constitution. We have come here peacefully and should earn respect around the world. I hope this will help maintain its goal is to protect the rights each state already had before joining the Union. The peaceful way we have reached this point should earn respect around the world, and I hope this will help maintain and improve us as we face challenges.

We based our decision to separate on our understanding of our rights and our desire to protect them. If that is correct, then our new Constitution will guide us to run a fair government that guarantees citizens' rights. Our success will prove we were right and that is the best way to make sure we have a peaceful relationship with the states who chose to remain.

If we were wrong, though, and we are unable to govern ourselves, then our experiment will fail. But if we're right, we'll experiment will fail; but if we are right, a prosperous future is before us, and we will have proved the capacity of the people for self-government. We have entered upon our career with no hostility to others, and with no desire to injure any. We have no purpose to invade, or to conquer, or to subjugate others. We are only acting on the defensive, and our sincere wish is for peace and free trade with all nations. If we cannot secure these by peaceful means, we will be compelled to arm in defense of our rights and liberties.

An agricultural people, whose chief interest is in the export of a commodity required in every manufacturing country, our true policy is peace and the freest trade which our necessities will permit. It is alike our interest and that of all those to whom we would sell and from whom we would buy, that there should be the fewest practicable restrictions upon the interchange of commodities.

There can be but little rivalry between ours and any manufacturing or navigating community, such as the Northeastern States of the American Union. It must

have a bright future, and our people will show they can govern themselves.

We have no wish to hurt anyone. We have no plans to invade or control other states or anyone else. We will defend ourselves, but we wish for peace. We want to continue trading with other nations including the Union. But if it comes to it, we will have to fight for our rights and freedom.

Our economy is based on agriculture, mainly selling crops needed for manufacturing. Our best policy is peace and free trade to support our own necessities. Both we and the nations we trade with benefit when there are as few trade restrictions as possible.

We don't want to compete with nations with a manufacturing or shipping economy like the Northeastern U.S. We have shared interests that can only be met by cooperating with each follow, therefore, that mutual interest would invite good will and kind offices. If, however, in spite of this, war should ensue, its events must develop the resources of the South and will stimulate the production of every article we require.

The necessities of war will stimulate the manufacture of arms and munitions, and the production of cloth and shoes and other articles of prime necessity; and the progress of the Confederacy will be placed beyond doubt.

It is an abuse of language to dignify a desire for peace as cowardice. The man who, in the consciousness of right, calmly awaits the result of an appeal to arms, if forced on him, is braver than he who seeks to avoid a contest by courting danger.

Our policy is peace, and the freest trade our necessities will permit. But if forced to take up arms, we will defend our rights and liberties to the last.

In our efforts to adjust our relations with our late associates in the Union, we have been willing to do everything which honor and self-respect permitted; but if this be refused

other. If war does come though, in spite of us trying to maintain peace, we will be forced to use our resources to provide what we need for defense.

War would encourage the creation of weapons, ammunition, clothing, shoes, and other essentials, meeting the Confederacy's needs.

We wish for peace. Calling that "cowardice" is wrong. There is nothing cowardly about working for peace rather than looking for someone or something to attack.

Our policy is peace and free trade, as far as our needs allow. But if we must fight, we will defend our rights and freedoms to the very end.

In trying to settle things peacefully with the Union, we have been willing to do everything we can while maintaining our honor. But if they refuse and force us into

us, and we are forced into conflict, the responsibility will rest upon those who deny us justice, not upon us.	war, the blame will be on them, not us.
Doubly justified by the absence of wrong on our part, and by wanton aggression on the part of others, there can be no cause to doubt the courage and patriotism of the people of the Confederate States, and it will be shown in every trial to which they may be called.	If we have done no wrong and others attack us without cause, we are justified. We know the courage and patriotism of the Confederate people, and they will show it in every challenge they face.
In the wisdom of the Almighty Ruler of the Universe I place my trust, and with humble reliance upon His goodness, I seek to perform the responsible duties of my station, trusting that He will guide me to a successful outcome.	I put my trust in God, and I will try to do my job faithfully, believing He will guide me to success.
I enter upon the duties of the office to which I have been chosen with a deep sense of the difficulties which lie before me, but with a firm faith in the strength and wisdom of the people and in the justice of our cause, and with an abiding hope that we may be permitted to live in peace with all mankind.	I take on my role knowing the difficulties ahead, but I firmly believe in the strength and wisdom of our people, in the justice of our cause, and in the hope that we can live in peace with everyone.

As an experienced soldier and politician, Jefferson Davis was certain of his beliefs and was not filled with his own importance. He was smart, respected, and committed to the cause of the

Confederacy. All this made him an ideal choice as President. However, not everyone in the South supported him. Some saw him as too proud and too stubborn. He was not able to unite the entire South, but there is no reason to believe anyone else could have done better.

As things turned out, the Confederate States of America had a relatively short history. Issues and events were seen very differently by the North and South. The following timeline charts the CSA's history and notes the differences in how they were viewed.

Dates	Confederate View	Union View
February 8, 1861	Delegates from seven seceded states met in Montgomery, Alabama and formed the Confederate States of America.	Seven states illegally broke away from the Union. They met in Montgomery, Alabama and formed a rebel government.
February 18, 1861	Jefferson Davis is inaugurated as the President of the Confederate States of America.	Jefferson Davis becomes the leader of the rebellion against the United States.
April 12, 1861	Confederate forces fire on Fort Sumter, beginning the war to defend Southern independence.	Rebels attack Fort Sumter, beginning an armed insurrection against the United States.
1861-1865	The Confederacy operates as an independent nation with its own president, congress, and military.	Rebels control parts of the South. The Union never recognizes it as legitimate.
April 9, 1865	General Robert E. Lee surrenders the Army of Northern Virginia at Appomattox, signaling an end to the war.	The surrender at Appomattox signals the end of the armed rebellion.

May 5, 1865	The Confederate government officially dissolves in Washington, Georgia and ceases to exist.	The United States resumes control over the South and the rebellion disbands.

Wrap Up

Jefferson Davis must have felt like a man with a target painted on his back. As the leader of a rebellion, or the leader of a new nation, depending on your perspective, he stood courageously in the public eye and spoke frankly about the wish for peace but the willingness to wage war.

Both Lincoln and Davis stood firm in their beliefs, and both promised to try to keep the peace. Each pointed at the other and said that if battles were to happen, it would be the other's fault and that they would not be the ones to start it.

Davis's presidency was one of duty, not his own personal goals. His promise was to do his best, not that he would be the best man for the job. He was committed but probably scared (not in a cowardly way) because he knew the heavy sacrifice that would be demanded of everyone if he failed to broker peace.

Yet, he was ready to lead, come Hell or high water. And they came.

Chapter 5: Laying Down the Law: Constitution of the Confederate States of America

March 11, 1861

The Confederate Constitution gives us a look into the beliefs and values of the Confederate States. Its structure was very much like the U.S. Constitution, but it was more than just a legal document about forming a new country. It also outlined the priorities and ideas the Confederate States would be guided by.

First and foremost, the Confederate Constitution protected every free person's right to own slaves. As it describes, slavery was the "cornerstone" of the new nation. This means it was the foundation on which the economy and culture would run. Not only was the practice of slavery protected, but Confederate states also were <u>not allowed</u> to ban slavery in their own states if they should ever decide they wanted to.

The Confederate Constitution placed more power in the hands of states than in the hands of the central government about slavery and other issues as well.

The following paragraphs show the Confederate Constitution in the original and modern languages. For a side-by-side comparison of the major ideas behind the United States Constitution and the Confederate Constitution, see Bonus Chapter 1.

The Confederate Constitution

ORIGINAL LANGUAGE	MODERN LANGUAGE
Preamble	
We, the people of the Confederate States, each State acting in its sovereign and independent character, in order to form a permanent federal government, establish justice,	We, the people of the Confederate States, each of us acting as a free and independent state, create a permanent federal government to guarantee justice, peace, and liberty for

insure domestic tranquility, and secure the blessings of liberty to ourselves and our posterity—invoking the favor and guidance of Almighty God—do ordain and establish this Constitution for the Confederate States of America.

ourselves and future generations, asking for God's guidance. We now establish this Constitution for the Confederate States of America.

Article I – Legislative Branch, Section 1. Congress

All legislative powers herein delegated shall be vested in a Congress of the Confederate States, which shall consist of a Senate and House of Representatives.

Lawmaking power belongs to the Confederate Congress, made up of two houses: the Senate and the House of Representatives.

Article I – Legislative Branch, Section 2. House of Representatives

The House of Representatives shall be composed of members chosen every second year by the people of the several States; and the electors in each State shall be citizens of the Confederate States, and have the qualifications requisite for electors of the most numerous branch of the State Legislature; but no person of foreign birth, not a citizen of the Confederate States, shall be allowed to vote for any officer, civil or political, State or Federal.

Every two years, people in each state will vote for who will be in the federal House of Representatives. To vote, a person has to be a Confederate citizen and follow the same rules as voters in their state's biggest law-making group. People who were born in another country and are not citizens are not allowed to vote in any state or national election.

No person shall be a Representative who shall not have attained the age of twenty-five years, and be a citizen of the Confederate States, and who shall not, when elected, be an inhabitant of that State in which he shall be chosen.

Representatives must be at least 25 years old, be Confederate citizens, and live in the state they represent.

Representatives and direct taxes shall be apportioned among the several States … according to their respective numbers … which shall be determined by adding to the whole number of free persons … three-fifths of all slaves.

The number of representatives and the amount of direct taxes each state gets will be based on how many people live in each state. To count the population, each free person counts as one and each slave as three-fifths of a person.

The actual enumeration shall be made within three years … and within every subsequent term of ten years …

A formal counting of the number of people (a census), will occur within three years and every ten years after that to determine how many representatives are approved for each state.

The number of Representatives shall not exceed one for every fifty thousand … but each State shall have at least one Representative; and until such enumeration shall be made, the State of South Carolina shall be entitled to six; Georgia ten; Alabama nine; Mississippi seven; Louisiana six; and Texas six.

The most representatives a state can have is one Representative per 50,000 people. Each state gets at least one Representative. Until the first census, specific numbers are assigned to the states that left the Union before this constitution was written: South Carolina, 6; Georgia, 10; Alabama, 9; Mississippi, 7; Louisiana, 6; and Texas, 6.

When vacancies happen … the executive authority thereof shall issue writs of election to fill such vacancies.	State governors must call special elections to fill vacancies in the House.

Article I – Legislative Branch, Section 3. Senate

The Senate of the Confederate States shall be composed of two Senators from each State, chosen for six years by the Legislature thereof; and each Senator shall have one vote.	Each state voting body chooses two Senators to serve six-year terms. Each Senator gets one vote.
Immediately after they shall be assembled … they shall be divided as equally as may be into three classes … so that one-third may be chosen every second year.	Senators are divided into three groups so that one-third are up for election every two years.
No person shall be a Senator who shall not have attained the age of thirty years and be a citizen of the Confederate States; and who shall not, when elected, be an inhabitant of the State for which he shall be chosen.	Senators must be at least 30 years old, Confederate citizens, and live in the state they represent.
The Vice President of the Confederate States shall be President of the Senate, but shall have no vote, unless they be equally divided.	The Vice President presides over the Senate but can only vote to break a tie.
The Senate shall choose their other officers … and also a	The Senate elects its own officers and a temporary leader

President pro tempore, in the absence of the Vice President ...	when the Vice President is absent.
The Senate shall have the sole power to try impeachments. ... no person shall be convicted without the concurrence of two-thirds of the members present.	Only the Senate may hold a trial when the government accuses an elected official of breaking the law or abusing their power (impeachment). Two-thirds of the Senators must vote to impeach the accused individual for them to be convicted.
Judgment in cases of impeachment shall not extend further than to removal from office, and disqualification ... but the party convicted shall, nevertheless, be liable ... to indictment, trial, judgment, and punishment, according to law. Article I – Legislative Branch, Section 4. Congressional Elections	The impeached person could lose their job and might no longer be allowed to run for any other elected position. But convicted officials can also face criminal trial and penalties. Therefore, other punishments could also be sentenced.
The times, places, and manner of holding elections ... shall be prescribed in each State by the Legislature thereof ... but the Congress may at any time, by law, make or alter such regulations, except as to the times and places of choosing Senators.	State legislatures set the rules for congressional elections, but Congress can change them (except for when and where Senators are chosen).
Congress shall assemble at least once every year ... the first Monday in December, unless	Congress must meet at least once a year, starting the first Monday in December, unless another day is set by law.

they shall by law appoint a different day.

Article I – Legislative Branch, Section 5. Rules and Procedures of Congress

Each House shall be the judge of the elections, returns, and qualifications of its own members; and a majority of each shall constitute a quorum …

Each House decides if its members were properly elected and qualified, meaning that the election was fair, legal, and not tampered with. A majority must be present to go forward with congressional discussions and votes.

Each House may determine the rules of its proceedings, punish its members for disorderly behavior, and, with the concurrence of two-thirds, expel a member.

Each House sets its own rules, can punish disorderly members, and can expel a member with a two-thirds vote.

Each House shall keep a journal of its proceedings … and the yeas and nays … shall … be entered on the journal.

Both Houses must keep a record of their activities, and their votes must be made public when requested by one-fifth of the members.

Neither House, during the session of Congress, shall, without the consent of the other, adjourn for more than three days …

Neither House can take a break for more than three days without the agreement of the other House of Congress.

Article I – Legislative Branch, Section 6. Rights and Restrictions of Members

The Senators and Representatives ... shall receive a compensation for their services, to be ascertained by law ... and paid out of the Treasury of the Confederate States.	Senators and Representatives are paid by the Confederate Treasury, with amounts set by law.
They shall ... be privileged from arrest during their attendance ... except for treason, felony, or breach of the peace ...	Members of Congress cannot be arrested while attending congressional meetings unless they are accused of betraying their country (treason), a very serious crime (felony), or causing trouble like starting a riot (breach of the peace).
No Senator or Representative shall, during the time for which he was elected, be appointed to any civil office under the authority of the Confederate States ...	Members of Congress can't be employed by a federal agency during their elected term.
And no person holding any office under the Confederate States shall be a member of either House ...	No one holding a federal office can also serve in Congress at the same time.
Article I – Legislative Branch, Section 7. Revenue Bills and Presidential Role	
All bills for raising revenue shall originate in the House of Representatives; but the Senate may propose or concur with amendments as on other bills.	Tax bills must begin in the House, but may be reviewed by the Senate, which can suggest changes.

Every bill ... shall ... be presented to the President ... If he approve he shall sign it, but if not he shall return it with his objections ...	The President must sign bills into law or return them to Congress with objections (veto).
If ... not returned ... within ten days ... the same shall be a law ... unless Congress ... prevents its return ...	If the President doesn't sign or veto a bill within 10 days, it becomes law unless Congress is not in session.
The President may approve any appropriation and disapprove any other appropriation in the same bill ... and shall ... return it ...	The President has line-item veto power, meaning he can approve part of a spending bill but still reject specific items.

Section 8. Powers of Congress

Lists familiar U.S. powers: "To lay and collect taxes ... pay the debts ... provide for the common defense and general welfare ... borrow money ... regulate commerce ... coin money ... establish post offices ... declare war ... raise armies ..."	Congress can tax, borrow, regulate trade, run post offices, declare war, support armies and navies, and pass laws on other national matters.
No bounties shall be granted from the treasury; nor shall any duties or taxes on importations ... be laid to promote or foster any branch of industry.	Congress can't place a tax on imports to promote local industry or give extra money to domestic businesses.
Congress shall have power ... to prohibit the introduction of slaves from any State not a member of, or territory not belonging to, this Confederacy.	Congress can ban importing slaves from the U.S. states that are not in the Confederacy or from non-Confederate territories.

But no law denying or impairing the right of property in negro slaves shall be passed.

Section 9. Limits on Congress

Borrowed heavily from the U.S. Constitution: no bills of attainder, no ex post facto laws, no titles of nobility, etc.

Congress may not pass any law limiting the right of its citizens to own slaves.

Congress cannot hold someone responsible for breaking a law that did not exist when the person committed the action. It cannot pass a law singling out an individual for punishment without a trial. And it cannot give anyone a special or royal title.

No ... appropriations ... shall be for a longer term than two years.

Federal spending must be spelled out in detail as to what the money is being spent on. A spending bill can only be approved for up to two years.

No money shall be drawn from the treasury but in consequence of appropriations made by law ...

Money set aside by the government can only be approved for two years at a time and for the purpose described

Every law ... shall relate to but one subject, and that shall be expressed in the title.

Laws must cover only one subject and must be clearly stated in the title.

No ... duties or taxes ... to promote or foster any branch of industry ...

No taxes or tariffs may be imposed for the purpose of giving an advantage to any industry or company.

Congress shall appropriate no money from the treasury unless

The President must request money for specific purposes

60

... asked and estimated for by ... the President ...	and must estimate how much money will be needed for that purpose.

Section 10. Limits on the States

Borrowed much from the U.S. Constitution: no treaties, alliances, coining money, bills of credit, or titles of nobility.	States may not make treaties, coin money, issue paper money, or designate anyone as having special privileges or advantages.
No State shall ... impair the right of property in negro slaves. States also restricted from levying tariffs or duties without Congress's approval.	States cannot outlaw slavery. Every state must protect its citizens' right to own slaves. States can't impose tariffs or duties unless Congress consents.

Article II. Confederate Constitution - Executive Branch, Section 1. The President

The executive power shall be vested in a President of the Confederate States of America. He and the Vice President shall hold their offices for the term of six years; but the President shall not be re-eligible. The President and Vice President shall be elected as follows:	The President holds executive power. He and the Vice President serve for six years. The President may serve only one term with no possibility of reelection.
Each State shall appoint, in such manner as the Legislature thereof may direct, a number of electors equal to the whole number of Senators and Representatives ... but no	States appoint electors (like in the U.S. Electoral College system), equal to their total number of Senators and Representatives. Members of

Senator or Representative, or person holding an office of trust or profit under the Confederate States, shall be appointed an elector.

The electors shall meet in their respective States, and vote by ballot for President and Vice President, one of whom … shall not be an inhabitant of the same State with themselves … They shall make distinct lists of all persons voted for as President, and of all persons voted for as Vice President …

The President of the Senate shall … open all the certificates, and the votes shall then be counted. The person having the greatest number of votes for President shall be the President, if such number be a majority of the whole number of electors appointed …

If no person have such majority, then from the two highest numbers on the list, the House of Representatives shall immediately choose by ballot the President … but in choosing the President, the votes shall be taken by States, the representation from each State having one vote …

Congress and federal officials cannot serve as electors.

Electors meet in their states to vote for President and Vice President. Either the President or Vice President may not be from the same state as the elector. The electors must certify their votes for President and Vice President separately. They must keep a written record of the votes.

The Senate President counts the electoral votes. The candidate with a majority of the votes becomes President.

If no candidate gets a majority, the House votes for one of the top two, with each state delegation getting one vote.

The person having the greatest number of votes as Vice President shall be the Vice President ... if a majority of the whole number of electors appointed vote for him ... if no person have a majority, then from the two highest ... the Senate shall choose the Vice President ...

The Vice President is chosen the same way. If no majority, the Senate elects the Vice President from the top two.

But no person constitutionally ineligible to the office of President shall be eligible to that of Vice President of the Confederate States.

Anyone who is not eligible to be President is also not eligible to be Vice President.

The Congress may determine the time of choosing the electors, and the day on which they shall give their votes ...

Congress sets the date(s) of when they choose electors.

No person, except a natural-born citizen of the Confederate States, or a citizen thereof at the time of the adoption of this Constitution ... shall be eligible ...; neither shall any person be eligible who shall not have attained the age of thirty-five years, and been fourteen years a resident ...

To be President, a person must be a natural-born Confederate citizen (or a U.S. citizen at adoption), at least 35 years old, and a resident for at least 14 years.

In case of the removal of the President from office, or of his death, resignation, or inability ... the same shall devolve on the Vice President ... Congress may by law provide for the case

If the President dies, resigns, or is removed, the Vice President takes over. Congress may create a law to determine what happens if both President and Vice President cannot serve.

of removal, death, resignation, or inability both of the President and Vice President …

The President shall, at stated times, receive … a compensation … which shall neither be increased nor diminished during the period … and he shall not receive … any other emolument from the Confederate States, or any of them.

The President receives a set salary that cannot change during his term. He may not accept any other payment from the Confederate or state governments.

Before he enter on the execution of his office, he shall take the following oath or affirmation: 'I do solemnly swear (or affirm) that I will faithfully execute the office of President … and will … preserve, protect, and defend the Constitution of the Confederate States.'

The President must swear an oath to faithfully execute his office and to preserve, protect, and defend the Confederate Constitution.

Article II. Confederate Constitution - Executive Branch, Section 2. Presidential Powers

The President shall be commander-in-chief of the army and navy of the Confederate States, and of the militia of the several States, when called into the actual service of the Confederate States …

The President is commander-in-chief of the Confederate military and state militias when the militias are in Confederate service.

He may require the opinion, in writing, of the principal officer in each of the Executive Departments …	He may request written advice from cabinet members.
He shall have power to grant reprieves and pardons for offenses against the Confederate States, except in cases of impeachment.	He may pardon offenders against Confederate law, except those impeached.
He shall have power, by and with the advice and consent of the Senate, to make treaties, provided two-thirds of the Senators present concur …	He may make treaties with the approval of two-thirds of Senators present.
He shall nominate, and, by and with the advice and consent of the Senate, shall appoint ambassadors, other public ministers and consuls, Judges of the Supreme Court, and all other officers …	He nominates and appoints ambassadors, ministers, consuls, Supreme Court justices, and other officers, with Senate approval.
The Congress may by law vest the appointment of such inferior officers … in the President alone, in the courts of law, or in the heads of departments.	Congress may let the President, courts, or department heads appoint minor officers.
The President shall have power to fill all vacancies that may happen during the recess of the Senate, by granting commissions … which shall expire at the end of their next session.	He may fill vacant offices in the Senate during recesses, but those appointments expire at the next Senate session.

Article II. Confederate Constitution - Executive Branch, Section 3. Presidential Duties

He shall from time to time give to the Congress information of the state of the Confederacy, and recommend to their consideration such measures as he shall judge necessary ...	He gives Congress updates on the Confederacy and recommends laws.
He may, on extraordinary occasions, convene both Houses ... and in case of disagreement ... he may adjourn them ...	He may call Congress into special session. If the House and Senate disagree he may cancel the session.
He shall receive ambassadors and other public ministers.	He officially receives foreign diplomats.
He shall take care that the laws be faithfully executed and shall commission all the officers of the Confederate States.	He must ensure laws are obeyed and must give official authority to Confederate officers (commissioning).

Article II. Confederate Constitution - Executive Branch, Section 4. Impeachment

The President, Vice President, and all civil officers of the Confederate States, shall be removed from office on impeachment for, and conviction of, treason, bribery,	The President, Vice President, and all federal officials may be removed from office if impeached and convicted for treason, bribery, felony other major crimes.

or other high crimes and misdemeanors.	

Wrap Up

The strong focus on slavery in the Confederate Constitution presumed the southern economy would continue to be primarily agriculture-based and would have an ongoing need for slaves. While the north also included a great deal of agriculture at the time, the economy was more diverse, with industry growing rapidly. This made the North somewhat less dependent on slavery, but it still needed it to some extent. This is especially true when you consider that products needed by the North's industries got their raw materials from the South, where they were produced by slaves. For example, Northern textile mills needed Southern cotton.

Some historians in today's conversations and debates about the Confederacy say the secession of eleven states was about many things, with slavery being only one of them. A look at the CSA Constitution, however, shows that while slavery may be only one of several issues, it is the top priority for the South to address.

Over the next four years, beginning with the Confederate attack on Fort Sumter, many bloody battles were fought, and many lives were lost or destroyed. Bonus Chapter 2 shows a summary of the major battles of the Civil War.

Chapter 6: Lincoln Changes His Tune: The Emancipation Proclamation

January 1, 1863

You may refer back to Abraham Lincoln's First Inaugural Address where he plainly stated that his goal was to preserve the Union and not to end nor preserve slavery. "I have no purpose, directly or indirectly, to interfere with the institution of slavery in the States where it exists." He reinforced his intention in August of 1862 in a letter to Horace Greeley, editor of the New York Tribune, where he said:

> "My paramount object in this struggle is to save the Union and is not either to save or destroy slavery.

> If I could save the Union without freeing any slave, I would do it, and if I could save it by freeing all the slaves, I would do it; and if I could save it by freeing some and leaving others alone, I would also do that."

However, by 1863, Lincoln came to see ending slavery as key to ending the war, and as both a military necessity and a moral duty.

Lincoln issued the Emancipation Proclamation on January 1, 1863. In it, Lincoln declared that all enslaved people living in the states that were fighting against the United States (the Confederacy) were now free. While it only ended slavery in Confederate states and not in states loyal to the Union, it was a major turning point in the war. It made the Civil War not only a fight to save the Union, but also a fight to end slavery. It also allowed freed slaves to join the Union Army and Navy, which added strength to the Union's cause. The Emancipation Proclamation paved the way for the eventual ending (abolition) of slavery throughout the entire country.

Chronologically, the Emancipation Proclamation was issued after the Battle of Antietam and before Vicksburg or Gettysburg. It came more than 2 years before the Confederate surrender at Appomattox.

Here is the Emancipation Proclamation written in modern language to make it more understandable to modern readers.

The Emancipation Proclamation

ORIGINAL LANGUAGE	MODERN LANGUAGE
By the President of the United States of America: A Proclamation.	An Official Statement from the President of the United States
Whereas, on the twenty-second day of September, in the year of our Lord one thousand eight hundred and sixty-two, a proclamation was issued by the President of the United States, containing, among other things, the following, to wit:	On September 22, 1862, I, the President of the United States, issued a statement that included the following points:
That on the first day of January, in the year of our Lord one thousand eight hundred and sixty-three, all persons held as slaves within any State, or designated part of a State, the people whereof shall then be in rebellion against the United States, shall be then, thenceforward, and forever free; and the Executive Government of the United States, including the military and naval authority thereof, will recognize and maintain the freedom of such persons, and will do no act or acts to repress such persons, or any of them, in any efforts they	Beginning January 1, 1863, all slaves in the states or parts of states that are rebelling against the United States will be free forever. The U.S. government, including the Army and Navy, will recognize and defend their freedom and will not act against any efforts they make to stay free.

may make for their actual freedom.

That the Executive will, on the first day of January aforesaid, by proclamation, designate the States and parts of States, if any, in which the people thereof, respectively, shall then be in rebellion against the United States; and the fact that any State, or the people thereof, shall on that day be, in good faith, represented in the Congress of the United States by members chosen thereto at elections wherein a majority of the qualified voters of such State shall have participated, shall, in the absence of strong countervailing testimony, be deemed conclusive evidence that such State, and the people thereof, are not then in rebellion against the United States.

Now, therefore I, Abraham Lincoln, President of the United States, by virtue of the power in me vested as Commander-in-Chief, of the Army and Navy of the United States in time of actual armed rebellion against the authority and government of the United States, and as a fit and necessary war measure for suppressing said rebellion, do, on this first day of January, in the year of our Lord one

I said earlier that on January 1, 1863, I would officially announce which states or parts of states are in rebellion. If a state is sending representatives to Congress, chosen by a majority of its eligible voters, then it will be considered not in rebellion unless there is strong proof to the contrary.

Today is January 1, 1863, and using my authority as Commander-in-Chief, I officially declare the following states to be in rebellion against the United States. I do this because I believe this is a necessary step to end the war.

thousand eight hundred and sixty-three, and in accordance with my purpose so to do, publicly proclaimed for the full period of one hundred days from the day first above mentioned, order and designate as the States and parts of States wherein the people thereof respectively, are this day in rebellion against the United States, the following, to wit:

Arkansas, Texas, Louisiana (except the Parishes of St. Bernard, Plaquemines, Jefferson, St. John, St. Charles, St. James Ascension, Assumption, Terrebonne, Lafourche, St. Mary, St. Martin, and Orleans, including the City of New Orleans), Mississippi, Alabama, Florida, Georgia, South Carolina, North Carolina, and Virginia (except the forty-eight counties designated as West Virginia, and also the counties of Berkeley, Accomack, Northampton, Elizabeth City, York, Princess Ann, and Norfolk, including the cities of Norfolk and Portsmouth), and which excepted parts, are for the present, left precisely as if this proclamation were not issued.

And by virtue of the power, and for the purpose aforesaid, I do

The states in rebellion are: Arkansas, Texas, Louisiana (except certain parishes including New Orleans), Mississippi, Alabama, Florida, Georgia, South Carolina, North Carolina, and Virginia (except for the 48 counties that would become West Virginia, and a few other counties and cities). These excluded areas are not affected by this order and remain unchanged. (Tennessee was not named as being in rebellion because at the time of the Emancipation Proclamation, the Union had already regained control over Tennessee.)

Using the authority mentioned earlier, I now declare that all order and declare that all persons held as slaves within said designated States, and parts of States, are, and henceforward shall be free; and that the Executive government of the United States, including the military and naval authorities thereof, will recognize and maintain the freedom of said persons.

And I hereby enjoin upon the people so declared to be free to abstain from all violence, unless in necessary self-defense; and I recommend to them that, in all cases when allowed, they labor faithfully for reasonable wages.

And I further declare and make known, that such persons of suitable condition, will be received into the armed service of the United States to garrison forts, positions, stations, and other places, and to man vessels of all sorts in said service.

And upon this act, sincerely believed to be an act of justice, warranted by the Constitution, upon military necessity, I invoke the considerate judgment of mankind, and the gracious favor of Almighty God.

In witness whereof, I have hereunto set my hand and

slaves in those designated states and parts of states are free, and the U.S. government, including the Army and Navy, will protect and maintain their freedom.

I advise those who are freed to avoid violence unless it is for self-defense. I also encourage them, whenever possible, to work honestly for fair pay.

I also announce that former slaves who are able may join the United States armed forces to help guard forts, hold positions, and serve on ships.

I truly believe this act is both needed to end the war and support the Constitution. I ask for the fair judgment of the world and the blessing of Almighty God.

To show my support of this, I have signed my name and had

caused the seal of the United States to be affixed.	the seal of the United States placed here.
Done at the City of Washington, this first day of January, in the year of our Lord one thousand eight hundred and sixty-three, and of the Independence of the United States of America the eighty-seventh.	Signed in Washington, D.C., on January 1, 1863, the eighty-seventh year of America's independence.
By the President: ABRAHAM LINCOLN	Signed, President Abraham Lincoln
WILLIAM H. SEWARD, Secretary of State.	Attested by Secretary of State William H. Seward

Wrap Up

At last, the words many had been waiting to hear! All slaves in the Confederacy are now free! Read that again. All slaves *in the Confederacy* are now free. The Emancipation Proclamation did not free slaves being held in Union or Border states. Many, possibly most, Confederate slave owners were not necessarily of a mind to simply release their slaves, and even if they wanted to, most could not afford to begin paying them.

In terms of changing hearts and minds, the Emancipation Proclamation, issued by the Union but aimed at the Confederacy, had about as much practical impact as France or China passing a law and telling the United States it had to obey that law. In other words, since the South declared themselves independent, it felt no reason to obey a law from the North.

Add to that, most slaves were uneducated, had no skills other than what they were assigned to by their former owners, had nowhere to go, and no way to make a living. There was no plan in place to help the slaves transition to a free life.

While the Proclamation was symbolically important, it also shifted the focus of the war from just preserving the Union to ending slavery. It allowed former slaves to join the military, which encouraged slaves who were not released by their owners to rebel or escape, and it also added to the Union's military strength. It didn't free all slaves immediately like flipping a switch, but it changed the conversation and the direction for the future.

Chapter 7: Plans Change—Lincoln Gets Assistance in Making Emancipation Real

Once freed or escaped former slaves began joining the Union Army, discrimination became readily apparent. With less pay, a disproportionate amount of undesirable assignments, and general poor treatment, these soldiers were expected to risk their lives alongside their white counterparts at a significant disadvantage.

Enter Frederick Douglass. Serving as an army recruiter for Black regiments, Douglass was determined to bring attention—and change—to the unequal treatment.

On August 10, 1863, Douglass attended a meeting at the White House in the hope of gaining the President's ear. No fan of Lincoln, Douglass was nevertheless impressed and felt real change may be possible.

"When I plead for recruits, I want to do it with my heart without qualification. I cannot do that now." Thus motivated, Douglass pursued and evolved a relationship, some might even say a partnership, with Lincoln.

A second meeting took place on August 29, 1864. The purpose was in response to Lincoln's request that Douglass help him write a plan to aid as many slaves as possible in escaping from the Confederacy. With re-election approaching, Lincoln was not at all certain of a second term. As the Republican prospects improved with the capture of Atlanta and other landmark Union victories, the plan was never implemented, but Lincoln and Douglass continued their cooperative relationship.

Douglass's Correspondence to Lincoln, August 29, 1864

ORIGINAL LANGUAGE	MODERN LANGUAGE
Sir: Since the interview with wh. Your Excellency was pleased to honor me a few days ago, I have	Sir: Since we met recently, I have been talking to other trustworthy men regarding your

freely conversed with several trustworthy and Patriotic Colored men concerning your suggestion that something should be speedily done to inform the slaves in the Rebel states of the true state of affairs in relation to them sho and to warn them as to what will be their probable condition should peace be concluded while they remain within the Rebel lines: and more especially to urge upon them the necessity of making their escape. All with whom I have thus far spoken on the subject, concur in the wisdom and benevolence of the Idea, and some of them think it practicable. That every slave who escapes from the Rebel states is a loss to the Rebellion and a gain to the Loyal Cause, I need not stop to argue the proposition is self evident. The negro is the stomach of the rebellion. I will therefore briefly submit at once to your Excellency — the ways and means by which many such persons may be wrested from the enemy and brought within our lines:	suggestion that we find a way to inform and warn slaves in the Confederacy about what to expect once the war ends, and to urge them to make their escape as soon as possible. I emphasized that every escape represents a loss to the rebellion and a gain for the Union. Those to whom I have spoken agree. Here is what we have come up with:
1st Let a general agt. be appointed by your Excellency charged with the duty of giving effect to your idea as indicated above: Let him have the means and power to employ twenty or	First, appoint a main organizer with a team of 20 or 25 others. Their duty will be to carry out your plan.

twenty five good men, having the cause at heart, to act as his agents: 2d Let these Agents which shall be selected by him, have permission to visit such points at the front as are most accessible to large bodies of slaves in the Rebel States: Let each of the said agts have power — to appoint one subagent or more in the locality where he may be required to operate: the said sub agent shall be thoroughly acquainted with the country — and well instructed as to the representations he is to make to the slaves: — but his cheif duty will be to conduct such squads of slaves as he may be able to collect, safely within the Loyal lines: Let the sub agents for this service be paid a sum not exceeding two dolls— per day while upon active duty.	Second, they should travel the front lines where they can reach large groups of slaves. They may each appoint a local assistant who knows the terrain and those helpers will be trained on what to say to the slaves. The helpers should be paid up to $2.00 while they are actively working.
3dly In order that these agents shall not be arrested or impeded in their work —let them be properly ordered to report to the General Commanding the several Departments they may visit, and recieve from them permission to pursue thier vocation unmolested. 4th Let provision be made that the slaves or Freed men thus brought within our lines shall receive subsistence until such of them as are fit shall enter the service of the Country or be	Third, these organizers and helpers should be given papers identifying them as legitimate agents of the Union. They should report to the commander of any department they visit to receive permission to proceed so they are not arrested or detained. Fourth, any slaves or free men brought to the Union side will be provided food and support until they are able to find jobs or join the Army.

otherwise employed and provided for: 5thly Let each agent appointed by the General agent be required to keep a strict acct of all his transactions, — of all monies recieved and paid out, of the numbers and the names of slaves brought into our lines under his auspices, of the plantations visited, and of everything properly connected with the prosecution of his work, and let him be required to make full reports of his proceedings — at least, once a fortnight to the General Agent.	Fifth, Organizers should keep a record of their activities including any money they spend, the names and number of slaves they bring behind Union lines, the plantations they visit, and anything else of relevance. They should send reports to the main organizer at least every two weeks.
6th Also, Let the General Agt be required to keep a strict acct of all his transactions with his agts and report to your Excellency or to an officer designated by you to recieve such reports. 7th Let the General Agt be paid a salary sufficient to enable him to employ a competant Clerk, and let him be stationed at Washington — or at some other Point where he can most readily receive communications from and send communications to his Agents: The General Agt should also have a kind of roving Commission within our lines, so that he may have a more direct and effective oversight of the whole work and thus ensure activity and	Sixth, the main organizer will keep accurate records from the reports he receives and will submit a report to you or to whoever you designate.

Seventh, the main organizer must receive a large enough salary so that he can hire a clerk. He should be based in Washington or another place where he can easily meet with and communicate with his assistants. He should also be able to travel freely within Union lines to oversee progress and ensure his assistants are effective. |

faithfulness on the part of his agents—	
This is but an imperfect outline of the plan — but I think it enough to give your Excellency an Idea of how the desirable work shall be executed. Your Obedient Servant Fredk Douglass	The plan is not perfect but I think it's close enough for us to get started. Sincerely, Frederick Douglass

Wrap Up

As noted earlier, Frederick Douglass was not an avid Lincoln supporter at first. Once they met and talked, and Lincoln took Douglass's concerns and advice seriously, their relationship warmed. Douglass realized the sense in Lincoln's stance of putting saving the Union before the entire annihilation of slavery. Had he preached the reverse, he would not have gained the support of many powerful Union supporters, without whom the uphill battle would have been even steeper.

While Lincoln professed to care not for whether slaves were freed, but only that the Union be preserved, Douglass began to see through his words and acknowledged Lincoln's true character. "Though Mr. Lincoln shared the prejudices of this white fellow-countrymen against the negro, it is hardly necessary to say that in his heart of hearts he loathed and hated slavery."

Chapter 8: A Sad Day for the North and South: The Gettysburg Address

November 19, 1863

In November 1863, President Abraham Lincoln gave a short but powerful speech at the dedication of a new cemetery in Gettysburg, Pennsylvania. Just a few months earlier, one of the war's bloodiest battles had been fought there, with tens of thousands of soldiers killed, wounded, or missing.

Lincoln's speech, known as the **Gettysburg Address**, came at a time when the nation was deeply divided and struggling to see a path forward. In just a little over two minutes, he reminded Americans why the United States was founded — on the belief that all people are created equal — and challenged them to make sure that the Union soldiers who died had not given their lives in vain.

He urged the living to dedicate themselves to finishing the work the fallen soldiers had begun: preserving the Union and ensuring that the country would have a "new birth of freedom" — a future where democracy ("government of the people, by the people, for the people") would survive and thrive.

Here is the Gettysburg Address written in modern language to make it more understandable to modern readers.

The Gettysburg Address

ORIGINAL LANGUAGE	MODERN LANGUAGE
Four score and seven years ago our fathers brought forth on this continent, a new nation, conceived in Liberty, and dedicated to the proposition that all men are created equal.	Eighty-seven years ago, our ancestors started a new nation here in America. They built it on the idea of freedom and the belief that all people are created equal.
Now we are engaged in a great civil war, testing whether that	Today we are in the middle of a terrible Civil War. This war will

nation, or any nation so conceived and so dedicated, can long endure.

We are met on a great battlefield of that war. We have come to dedicate a portion of that field, as a final resting place for those who here gave their lives that that nation might live. It is altogether fitting and proper that we should do this.

But, in a larger sense, we can not dedicate—we can not consecrate—we can not hallow—this ground. The brave men, living and dead, who struggled here, have consecrated it, far above our poor power to add or detract.
The world will little note, nor long remember what we say here, but it can never forget what they did here.

It is for us the living, rather, to be dedicated here to the unfinished work which they who fought here have thus far so nobly advanced.
It is rather for us to be here dedicated to the great task remaining before us—that from these honored dead we take increased devotion to that cause for which they gave the last full measure of devotion—that we here highly resolve that these

decide whether our nation, or any nation built on these principles, can survive.

We are gathered on this battlefield to dedicate part of it as a cemetery for the soldiers who died here so that our nation could live on. We believe this is the right thing to do.

We know our words cannot make this ground sacred. The brave soldiers who fought here, both living and dead, have already made it sacred by their sacrifice, beyond anything we can do.

People may not remember what we say here today, but they will never forget what the soldiers did here.

It is up to us, the living, to continue the important work that these soldiers so bravely carried forward.

We must commit ourselves to the work we still need to do: to be inspired by the sacrifice of these soldiers, who gave their lives for this cause. We must promise that they did not die for nothing, that our nation, with God's help, will have new

dead shall not have died in vain—that this nation, under God, shall have a new birth of freedom—and that government of the people, by the people, for the people, shall not perish from the earth.	freedom, and that democracy, a government of the people, run by the people and for the people, will never disappear from the earth.

Wrap Up

Abraham Lincoln's speech was short. It only took him about two minutes to deliver it. Yet it is known as one of the most powerful speeches in the history of the United States. In just a few paragraphs, Lincoln summarized the purpose and the horror of the war and captured people's minds about the great sacrifices being made for a great cause. He enlisted people to continue to work hard towards a lasting peace so that the soldiers would not have given their lives for nothing.

The Gettysburg Address validated what Lincoln had said all along: that protecting the Union was a goal, maybe the most important goal, that was worth fighting for.

Chapter 9: Making It Official: The Thirteenth Amendment to the United States Constitution – Abolition of Slavery

January 31, 1865

     Lincoln recognized that the Emancipation Proclamation, which he issued on January 1, 1863, was an important step but did not go far enough. By 1864, Lincoln began to push for the passage of an amendment to the Constitution that would end slavery in all U.S. states and territories, calling it a great step toward freedom and justice. The groundwork he laid led to the passage of the amendment on January 31, 1865.

     The 13th Amendment to the United States Constitution officially ended slavery everywhere in the United States. It made it illegal to own or force someone to work as a slave anywhere in the country, except as punishment for a crime after a proper trial. This amendment was the first of the three "Reconstruction Amendments" added after the Civil War, and it put into law the freedom that the Emancipation Proclamation had promised. By passing the 13th Amendment, the United States permanently did away with slavery and took a major step toward creating a nation based on freedom and equal rights for everyone.

     Here is the short but powerful 13th Amendment to the Constitution, written in modern language to make it more understandable to modern readers.

The Thirteenth Amendment to the U.S. Constitution

ORIGINAL LANGUAGE	MODERN LANGUAGE
Section 1	
Neither slavery nor involuntary servitude, except as a punishment for crime whereof the party shall have been duly	Slavery and forced labor are not allowed anywhere in the United States or its territories. The only exception is when a person has

convicted, shall exist within the United States, or any place subject to their jurisdiction.	been found guilty of a crime through a fair trial in a court of law. Then they can be required to work as part of their punishment.
Section 2 Congress shall have power to enforce this article by appropriate legislation.	Congress has the authority to make laws that ensure this amendment is obeyed and carried out.

Wrap Up

After the Gettysburg Address, the Union gained new momentum. Ulysses S. Grant was appointed commander of all Union armies in March of 1864, and his focus was on defeating Confederate forces wherever they were. Aggressive military tactics were put to use, such as Sherman's March to the Sea in 1864 and the Siege of Richmond in early 1865.

With former slaves enlisting in Union forces, the army and navy got stronger, and as the Union took control over more of the South through military victories, more slaves were freed to contribute even more. The growth of Union strength was like a snowball rolling downhill, gathering more speed and intensity as it progressed. Lincoln pushed hard for the Emancipation Proclamation to be reinforced by law and urged Congress to do so.

The result of his efforts was the passage of the 13th Amendment to the Constitution of the United States, which was ratified (agreed to and made official) on December 6, 1865. Abraham Lincoln did not live to see its passage.

Chapter 10: Lincoln's Second Inaugural Address

March 4, 1865

Abraham Lincoln was reelected as President in 1864. In March 1865, as the Civil War was coming to an end, he delivered his Second Inaugural Address before once again taking office. The nation had been at war for four long and bloody years, and everyone hoped peace was near. Unlike his first inaugural speech, where he explained his plans for the country, this speech was short, serious, and very thoughtful of what everyone had been through.

Lincoln spoke honestly about the causes of the war, especially slavery, and recognized the heavy toll it had taken on both North and South. He suggested that the war might be God's punishment for the sin of slavery, and he called on Americans not to seek revenge, but instead to heal the nation.

With his famous words, **"With malice toward none; with charity for all,"** Lincoln urged the country to come together, care for soldiers and their families, and work for a lasting peace after the conflict ended.

Abraham Lincoln's Second Inaugural Address

ORIGINAL LANGUAGE	MODERN LANGUAGE
At this second appearing to take the oath of the Presidential office there is less occasion for an extended address than there was at the first. Then a statement, somewhat in detail, of a course to be pursued seemed fitting and proper. Now, at the expiration of four years, during which public declarations have been constantly called forth on every point and phase of the great	Now that I'm taking the oath of office for the second time, I don't need to give a long speech like I did the first time. Four years ago, it made sense to explain in detail what I planned to do. But after four years of a terrible war, with constant public discussion about every part of it, there's little new I can add. Everyone knows the progress of our military, and I hope the nation finds it

contest which still absorbs the attention and engrosses the energies of the nation, little that is new could be presented. The progress of our arms, upon which all else chiefly depends, is as well known to the public as to myself; and it is, I trust, reasonably satisfactory and encouraging to all. With high hope for the future, no prediction in regard to it is ventured.

On the occasion corresponding to this four years ago, all thoughts were anxiously directed to an impending civil war. All dreaded it, all sought to avert it. While the inaugural address was being delivered from this place, devoted altogether to saving the Union without war, insurgent agents were in the city seeking to destroy it without war—seeking to dissolve the Union, and divide effects, by negotiation. Both parties deprecated war, but one of them would make war rather than let the nation survive, and the other would accept war rather than let it perish. And the war came.

One-eighth of the whole population were colored slaves, not distributed generally over the Union, but localized in the

encouraging. I won't make predictions, but I have hope for the future.

Four years ago, at my first inauguration, everyone worried about the threat of civil war. We all wanted to avoid it. Even as I was speaking about saving the Union peacefully, representatives from the South were here in Washington trying to break it apart peacefully. Both sides said they didn't want war, but the South was willing to start one to destroy the Union, and the North was willing to fight to preserve it. And so, the war began.

At the start of the war, about one-eighth of the U.S. population were slaves, mostly in the South. Slavery was a huge

Southern part of it. These slaves constituted a peculiar and powerful interest. All knew that this interest was somehow the cause of the war. To strengthen, perpetuate, and extend this interest was the object for which the insurgents would rend the Union, even by war; while the Government claimed no right to do more than to restrict the territorial enlargement of it. Neither party expected for the war, the magnitude, or the duration, which it has already attained. Neither anticipated that the cause of the conflict might cease with, or even before, the conflict itself should cease. Each looked for an easier triumph, and a result less fundamental and astounding.

Both read the same Bible and pray to the same God; and each invokes His aid against the other. It may seem strange that any men should dare to ask a just God's assistance in wringing their bread from the sweat of other men's faces; but let us judge not, that we be not judged. The prayers of both could not be answered—that of neither has been answered fully. The Almighty has His own purposes. "Woe unto the world because of offenses! for it must

and powerful issue, and everyone knew it was the cause of the war. The South went to war to protect and expand slavery, while the Union only wanted to stop it from spreading. Neither side thought the war would last this long or be this horrible. Neither imagined that slavery itself might end during the war. Both expected a quicker, easier victory and a less dramatic outcome.

Both sides read the same Bible and pray to the same God, each asking for His help against the other. It may seem strange that anyone would ask God to help them make a living by forcing others to be slaves, but we should not judge. God has not fully answered the prayers of either side, and He has His own purposes. The Bible says bad things will happen, but it won't go easy for the ones who cause them. If slavery is one of those offenses that God allowed for a needs be that offenses come; but woe to that man by whom the offense cometh!" If we shall suppose that American slavery is one of those offenses which, in the providence of God, must needs come, but which, having continued through His appointed time, He now wills to remove, and that He gives to both North and South this terrible war as the woe due to those by whom the offense came, shall we discern therein any departure from those divine attributes which the believers in a Living God always ascribe to Him? Fondly do we hope, fervently do we pray, that this mighty scourge of war may speedily pass away. Yet, if God wills that it continue until all the wealth piled by the bondman's two hundred and fifty years of unrequited toil shall be sunk, and until every drop of blood drawn with the lash shall be paid by another drawn with the sword, as was said three thousand years ago, so still it must be said "the judgments of the Lord are true and righteous altogether."

With malice toward none; with charity for all; with firmness in the right, as God gives us to see the right, let us strive on to finish the work we are in; to

time but now intends to end, then this terrible war may be His punishment on both North and South. We hope and pray the war will end soon. But if God wills it, it could continue until all the wealth earned by slavery over the last 250 years is gone and every drop of blood spilled by slavery practices or battle is wiped away, then we must accept that as God's righteous judgment.

Let us move forward without hatred, showing kindness to all. With determination to do what we believe is right, let us work to finish this war. Let's heal the

bind up the nation's wounds; to care for him who shall have borne the battle, and for his widow, and his orphan—to do all which may achieve and cherish a just and lasting peace among ourselves, and with all nations.	nation's wounds, care for the soldiers who fought, and support their widows and orphans. Above all, let us seek a fair and lasting peace for America and for the world.

Wrap Up

As eloquent a speaker as Abraham Lincoln was, his second inaugural address may be the most profound speech he ever gave. It wasn't long. In fact, he said in the speech that it didn't need to be long. He had a few things to say, and he said them with great feeling.

Perhaps the most famous line ever written in American history came near the end of the speech. Even though the Union was on the verge of winning the war, Lincoln did not speak as a victorious Commander-in-Chief. Instead, he spoke as a peacemaker and urged everyone else to think that way too.

"With malice toward none; with charity for all...; let us strive on to finish the work we are in; to bind up the nation's wounds; to care for him who shall have borne the battle, and for his widow, and his orphan – to do all which may achieve and cherish a just and lasting peace among ourselves, and with all nations."

In other words, Lincoln asked everyone not to treat the Union's former enemies with anger. Instead, he urged, let us all do everything we can to reunite our nation and take care of our people – ALL of our people.

Chapter 11: The War Finally Ends – The Generals' Correspondence

Confederate General Robert E. Lee and Union Lieutenant General Ulysses S. Grant exchanged letters over two days in April 1865. This correspondence forms the written record of the end of the Civil War through the surrender of the Army of Northern Virginia, which was the Confederacy's primary fighting force.

Grant received Lee's surrender and responded with respect. His terms were generous: Confederate soldiers could return home with their horses and personal sidearm, and they would not be prosecuted for treason. This was intended to help the nation heal and encourage peace.

Below is their correspondence:

Lee to Grant, April 8, 1865

ORIGINAL LANGUAGE	MODERN LANGUAGE
General: I received at a late hour your note of to-day. In mine of yesterday I did not intend to propose the surrender of the Army of Northern Virginia, but to ask the terms of your proposition.	General: I got your letter late last night. I wasn't offering to surrender but only meant to ask about the terms you would accept if surrender should happen.
To be frank, I do not think the emergency has arisen to call for the surrender of this army; but as the restoration of peace should be the sole object of all, I desired to know whether your proposals would lead to that end.	To be honest, I really don't believe the situation yet demands this army's surrender. But since peace should be everyone's ultimate goal, I wanted to know if your proposal could help achieve that.
I cannot, therefore, meet you with a view to surrender the	I will meet with you but not with a plan to surrender, but to

Army of Northern Virginia; but as far as your proposal may affect the Confederate States forces under my command, and tend to the restoration of peace, I should be pleased to meet you at 10 A.M. to-morrow on the old stage road to Richmond, between the picket-lines of the two armies. Very respectfully, Your obedient servant, R. E. Lee, General	see what you propose and how it will affect the Confederate States and my army. Most of all, I want to know how your plan will help restore peace. I will meet with you tomorrow at 10 a.m. on the old stage road to Richmond between the picket lines of the two armies. Very respectfully, Your obedient servant, R. E. Lee, General

Grant to Lee, April 8, 1865

ORIGINAL LANGUAGE	MODERN LANGUAGE
General R. E. Lee, Commanding C.S.A.: Your note of yesterday is received. As I have no authority to treat on the subject of peace, the meeting proposed for 10 A.M. to-day could lead to no good. I will state, however, General, that I am equally anxious for peace with yourself, and the whole North entertains the same feeling. The terms upon which peace can be had are well understood. By the South laying down their arms, they will hasten that most desirable event, save thousands of human lives, and hundreds of millions of property not yet destroyed.	General Lee: I received your letter from yesterday. Since I don't have the authority to negotiate peace, the meeting you suggested for 10 a.m. today wouldn't be productive. That said, I want you to know I want peace just as much as you do—and so does the entire North. The conditions for peace are already well understood: if the South lays down its arms, it will bring peace sooner, save thousands of lives, and prevent even more destruction of property.

Sincerely hoping that all our difficulties may be settled without the loss of another life, I subscribe myself, etc., U. S. Grant, Lieutenant-General	I truly hope we can resolve our conflict without losing another life. Sincerely, U.S. Grant, Lieutenant General

Lee to Grant, Request for a Meeting, Morning, April 9, 1865

ORIGINAL LANGUAGE	MODERN LANGUAGE
General: I received your note of this morning on the picket-line, whither I had come to meet you and ascertain definitely what terms were embraced in your proposal of yesterday with reference to the surrender of this army. I now request an interview in accordance with the offer contained in your letter of yesterday for that purpose. Very respectfully, Your obedient servant, R. E. Lee, General	General, I got your message this morning at the picket line, where I had come to meet you and find out exactly what surrender terms you meant in your letter yesterday. I'm now asking for a meeting, as you offered, to talk about surrendering this army. Respectfully, Your obedient servant, R. E. Lee, General

Grant's Reply, Late Morning, April 9, 1865

ORIGINAL LANGUAGE	MODERN LANGUAGE
General R.E. Lee, Commanding C.S.A: Your note of this date is but this moment, 11:50 a.m., received, in consequence of my having passed from the Richmond and Lynchburg Road	General Lee: I just got your message. It's now 11:50 a.m. I changed my route from the Richmond-Lynchburg Road to the Farmville-Lynchburg Road.

to the Farmville and Lynchburg Road.	
I am at this writing about four miles west of Walker's Church and will push forward to the front for the purpose of meeting you.	I'm currently about four miles west of Walker's Church and am moving forward to meet you.
Notice sent to me on this road where you wish the interview to take place will meet me.	Send word along this road with the location you'd like to meet, and it will reach me.
Very respectfully, Your obedient servant, U.S. Grant, Lieutenant General	Sincerely, U.S. Grant, Lieutenant General

Grant's Terms of Surrender, During the Meeting, April 9, 1865

ORIGINAL LANGUAGE	MODERN LANGUAGE
General: In accordance with the substance of my letter to you of the 8th inst., I propose to receive the surrender of the Army of Northern Virginia on the following terms, to wit:	General: In line with what I wrote you on April 8, I propose the following terms for the surrender of the Army of Northern Virginia:
Rolls of all the officers and men to be made in duplicate, one copy to be given to an officer designated by me, the other to be retained by such officer or officers as you may designate.	Lists of all officers and soldiers must be made in two copies—one will go to me, and the other stays with whoever you appoint.
The officers to give their individual paroles not to take up arms against the Government of the United States until	Officers will give their word (parole) not to fight against the U.S. again unless they're officially exchanged. Each

properly exchanged, and each company or regimental commander to sign a like parole for the men of their commands.	company or regiment leader will also give parole for the men under them.
The arms, artillery, and public property to be parked and stacked, and turned over to the officers appointed by me to receive them. This will not embrace the side-arms of the officers, nor their private horses or baggage.	All weapons, cannons, and government supplies must be gathered, stacked, and handed over to my officers. But this **does not** include officers' personal weapons, their own horses, or their baggage.
This done, each officer and man will be allowed to return to his home, not to be disturbed by United States authority so long as they observe their paroles and the laws in force where they may reside.	Once this is done, every officer and man can go home and will not be bothered by U.S. forces as long as they keep their word and follow the laws where they live.
Very respectfully, U. S. Grant, Lieutenant General	Respectfully, U. S. Grant, Lieutenant General

Lee's Acceptance of the Terms, Afternoon, April 9, 1865

ORIGINAL LANGUAGE	MODERN LANGUAGE
General: I received your letter of this date containing the terms of the surrender of the Army of Northern Virginia as proposed by you.	General, I received your letter today laying out the terms for surrendering the Army of Northern Virginia.
I have the honor to reply that I accept them.	I am honored to say that I accept those terms.
I will proceed to designate the proper officers to carry the stipulations into effect.	I will now assign the appropriate officers to carry out the agreement.

Very respectfully,	Respectfully,
Your obedient servant,	R. E. Lee, General
R. E. Lee, General	

Wrap Up

Something that stands out through all of the letters between Robert E. Lee and Ulysses S. Grant is the respectful way in which they spoke to each other. For two men who had spent the last few years leading armies in battle after battle, you might have thought they hated one another. But that was not the case. Each man was there to do a job that would facilitate a means to an end. In the one case, the end that was sought was the preservation of the Union; in the other case, the desired end was the preservation of Southern values, practices, and way of life. The fight was not personal.

If either general had treated the other condescendingly or disrespectfully, there is a high likelihood that either the war would not have ended at this point, or the reuniting of the Union would have been much more difficult. Both Grant and Lee were gentlemen who would not let that happen.

Chapter 12: The Aftermath of the War: Lincoln's Final Public Address

April 11, 1865

Once the war was officially over, President Lincoln made a public speech from the balcony of the White House. Crowds were gathering, and he wanted to celebrate the end of the war and talk about the reconstruction of the areas that had been the most damaged by violence. He also addressed the rights of former slaves, which shocked many people. John Wilkes Booth, the man who murdered the President just three days later, was in the audience and is supposed to have said, "That means n----- citizenship. That is the last speech he will ever make."

No one knew at that point how the South should be brought back into the Union. Lincoln leaned toward taking a forgiving approach and supporting Southern states that were already beginning to redesign their own laws like Louisiana.

Below is the full text of that speech in its original language, along with a modern translation to make it easier for modern readers to understand.

Lincoln's Last Message

ORIGINAL LANGUAGE	MODERN LANGUAGE
We meet this evening, not in sorrow, but in gladness of heart. The evacuation of Petersburg and Richmond, and the surrender of the principal insurgent army, give hope of a righteous and speedy peace, whose joyous expression can not be restrained. In the midst of this, however, He from whom all blessings flow must not be forgotten.	We're here tonight not to mourn, but to celebrate. The Confederate armies have surrendered major cities like Petersburg and Richmond, and their main army has given up. This gives us real hope that peace is near, and a good kind of peace. In our celebration, though, let's not forget to thank God, who gives us all good things.

Nor must those whose harder part gives us the cause of rejoicing be overlooked. Their honors must not be parceled out with others. I myself was near the front, and had the high pleasure of transmitting much of the good news to you.

But what next? I suppose it will be said that I am interfering with the government of Louisiana. The fact is, I am saving it from interference. In my view, the military should not set up governments.

When people set up a government, they have the right to do so, and to be recognized by others as having done so. If a state has loyal people, it has the right to govern itself.
Some twelve thousand voters in the heretofore slave-state of Louisiana have sworn allegiance to the Union, assumed control of their affairs, and held elections. The Legislature has taken steps to revise its laws to be in line with freedom. They are organizing schools, including for the black population. The question is whether the federal government should recognize this government.

And we shouldn't forget the people who did the hardest work to make this moment possible – the soldiers and those who supported them. I was near the front lines myself and had the great honor of bringing you much of this good news.

So, what comes next? Some may say I'm interfering in how Louisiana is being run. But really, I'm trying to stop others from interfering. I don't think the army should be setting up governments.

When people in a state set up a government for themselves, and they are loyal to the Union, they should be allowed to govern themselves and be recognized by the rest of the country.
In Louisiana, around 12,000 people have taken an oath to support the Union. They've started running their own government, held elections, and begun changing their laws to reflect freedom instead of slavery. They're even starting schools including for Black children. So, the big question is: Should we recognize this government?

It is not perfect — it does not yet give the right to vote to the colored man. I would prefer that it did. Yet the question is not whether it is perfect, but whether it is better than what we had before. If we reject it, we throw away something better than nothing.

I repeat, if we reject the Louisiana government, we do so without anything better in its place. I believe it is easier to improve a thing once started than to start something new from scratch.

In support of this view, I refer to a letter I wrote last year (which I still stand by), stating that while I was not committed to any particular form of reconstruction, I was committed to accepting governments formed by the people and for the people — so long as they were loyal to the Union and shaped by free elections.

In conclusion, we must recognize that we are shaping the future of the Union — not just for Louisiana, but for all the states in rebellion. Let us be careful and not throw away what progress has been made.

It's not a perfect government. It doesn't yet give former slaves the right to vote. I wish it did. But the real question is: Is it better than what existed before? I think it is. If we reject it, we throw away something that is better than nothing.

Again, rejecting it means we throw away something we could build on and improve. It's usually easier to fix something that's already been started than to build something new from scratch.

I said something similar in a letter last year, and I still believe it: I'm not tied to one way of rebuilding the Southern states, but I believe that if the people of a state form a loyal government through fair elections, it should be accepted.

Finally, we should remember that what we do now in Louisiana will affect how all the other rebellious states are brought back into the Union. We need to be wise and not waste the progress we've already made.

Wrap Up

In what would become his last words to the nation, Abraham Lincoln sent a message of hope, peace, and respect. Just as Generals Lee and Grant had recognized each other as professionals and fellow Americans during the surrender talks, Lincoln set the tone for others to do so as well. His aim was, as it always had been, to preserve the Union, and the best way to do that, he must have reasoned, was to treat the Southern secessionist states as returning family and not as rebels to be punished. His assassination a few days later most likely cemented that direction and tone into everyone's consciousness and became the operating principle of the Reconstruction era.

Chapter 13: Who Will Carry On? The Nation Mourns

April 14-15, 1865

Abraham Lincoln was shot on April 14, 1865 by John Wilkes Booth, an actor and Southern supporter, at Ford's Theater in Washington, D.C. He died the next morning on April 15.

In the days, weeks, and months that followed, many poems, documents, articles, and stories were written by people from many walks of life to commemorate his life and passing. One of the most famous was a poem by Walt Whitman, "When Lilacs Last in the Dooryard Bloom'd." The language of this very long poem is a reflection of the time in which it was written and may prove challenging for modern readers. While it never specifically mentions Lincoln by name, the meaning is clear in lines such as "…Comrades mine and I in the midst, and their memory ever to keep, for the dead I loved so well, for the sweetest, wisest soul of all my days and lands—and this for his dear sake…"

On April 14, 1865, Reverend Henry Ward Beecher, a well-known abolitionist preacher, was asked by the Union government to deliver a speech at Fort Sumter, which he did. The speech was to commemorate the 4 years since the Confederate attack on Fort Sumter, and the replacement of the Confederate flag with the Union flag over the fort. At the time of the address, those at the Fort Sumter event did not know Lincoln had been shot that day.

On April 25, 1865, President Andrew Johnson, the Vice President who was sworn in as President upon Lincoln's death, called for a national day of mourning on May 25. This allowed time for the word to spread that the President had been assassinated. Mourning activities included draping government buildings in black and citizens holding processions and prayer services at public gatherings. Lincoln was remembered as the savior of the Union and a martyr to the cause of liberty.

Johnson's Proclamation, known as Proclamation 129, follows in its original language and a modern language translation to help make it more understandable for modern readers.

Andrew Johnson's Proclamation Honoring Lincoln

ORIGINAL LANGUAGE	MODERN LANGUAGE
A Proclamation by the President of the United States of America.	An Executive Order of the President.
Whereas, by my direction, the Acting Secretary of State, in a notice to the public of the 17th, requested the various religious denominations to assemble on the 19th instant, on the occasion of the obsequies of Abraham Lincoln, late President of the United States, and to observe the same with appropriate ceremonies; but	On April 19, I directed the Acting Secretary of State and the religious leaders who were invited to gather for services honoring President Abraham Lincoln. But our whole nation is mourning, not just those few. I feel we need another special day to show respect to God and ask that this loss help make our country stronger.
Whereas our country has become one great house of mourning, where the head of the family has been taken away, and believing that a special period should be assigned for again humbling ourselves before Almighty God, in order that the bereavement may be sanctified to the nation:	Senators and Representatives have asked for this and therefore, I, Andrew Johnson, President of the United States, declare that Thursday, May 25, 1865, be observed wherever the American flag is given respect, as a Day of Mourning.
Now, therefore, in order to mitigate that grief on earth which can only be assuaged by communion with the Father in heaven, and in compliance with the wishes of Senators and	On that day, I ask all citizens to come together in their churches or wherever they worship. I ask that everyone unite in solemn, reverent services to remember the great man we've lost. May

Representatives in Congress, communicated to me by resolutions adopted at the National Capitol, I, Andrew Johnson, President of the United States, do hereby appoint Thursday, the 25th day of May next, to be observed, wherever in the United States the flag of the country may be respected, as a day of humiliation and mourning, and I recommend my fellow-citizens then to assemble in their respective places of worship, there to unite in solemn service to Almighty God in memory of the good man who has been removed, so that all shall be occupied at the same time in contemplation of his virtues and in sorrow for his sudden and violent end.

In witness whereof I have hereunto set my hand and caused the seal of the United States to be affixed.

Done at the city of Washington, the 25th day of April, A. D. 1865, and of the Independence of the United State of America the eighty-ninth.

ANDREW JOHNSON
By the President:
W. HUNTER
Acting Secretary of State

---

these gatherings help us reflect on his virtues and grieve a violent, tragic end.

I am signing this document and having it marked with the official seal of the United States.

Signed at the City of Washington on April, 25 1865.

Andrew Johnson, President of the United States
By the President: W. Hunter, Acting Secretary of State

On April 19, 1865, James A. Garfield, who was then a Member of Congress and later became President, delivered a speech on Lincoln at the U.S. Capitol during the official funeral.

The original text of Garfield's speech is below, along with a modern language translation to make it easier to understand for modern readers.

James Garfield's Speech to Congress Honoring Lincoln

ORIGINAL LANGUAGE	MODERN LANGUAGE
Mr. Speaker, I desire to move that this House do now adjourn. And before the vote upon that motion is taken I desire to say a few words.	Mr. Speaker, I ask that the House adjourn for the day. But before we vote on that, I would like to say a few words.
This day, Mr. Speaker, will be sadly memorable so long as this nation shall endure, which God grant may be "till the last syllable of recorded time," when the volume of human history shall be scaled up and delivered to the omnipotent Judge.	This day, Mr. Speaker, will always be remembered with sadness for as long as our country exists, which hopefully will be forever until all of human history is finished and judged by God.
In all future time, on the recurrence of this day, I doubt not that the citizens of this Republic will meet in solemn assembly to reflect on the life and character of Abraham Lincoln, and the awful tragic event of April 14, 1865—an event unparalleled in our own. It is eminently proper that this House should this day place	I believe Americans will honor Abraham Lincoln's life and character, and will remember the terrible tragedy of April 14, 1865, an event unlike any in our history. It's only right that we, in the House of Representatives, should officially record this as well.

upon its records a memorial of that event.

But greatest among all these great developments were the character and fame of Abraham Lincoln, whose loss the nation still deplores.	Above all the great things that we have seen in our time, the most powerful was the character and legacy of Abraham Lincoln. The nation will continue to mourn his loss deeply.
It was no one man who killed Abraham Lincoln;	Abraham Lincoln wasn't killed by just one person.
it was the embodied spirit of treason and slavery, inspired with fearful and despairing hate, that struck him down in the moment of the nation's supremest joy.	His death came about due to treason and slavery, which were driven by hate and fear at the very moment when our nation was celebrating its greatest victory.
Ah! Sir there are times in the history of men and nations when they stand so near the veil that separates mortals from the immortals ... the nation stood so near the veil that the whispers of God were heard by the children of men.	There are moments in human and national history when we come so close to the boundary between life and the afterlife… that we can almost feel the presence of something greater. In this moment of grief and sacrifice, our nation can almost hear the whispers of God.

Wrap Up

Likely, many in the South did not exactly mourn Abraham Lincoln's passing. But even they had to wonder how everyone would move forward. The war was over. Many areas lay in ruins. Families had lost their homes, lands, and businesses. And the North, victors in the war, was offering to help rebuild. They couldn't refuse and probably didn't want to.

The question was, now that Lincoln was gone, would Andrew Johnson and others keep the direction that Lincoln had set when he declared that the United States would continue on "with malice toward none and charity for all." It was time for everyone to move on together.

Conclusion: Understanding the Past, Shaping the Future

Think of the Civil War era as a test you forgot to study for. For eight decades, American citizens had been living life under the U.S. Constitution, which proclaimed freedom for all. While people were sharply divided as to exactly what that meant, free citizens still knew they could rely on that principle. As the 1800s wore on, many could feel the divide widening, but relatively few understood the country was headed toward tearing up the very Constitution under which they lived. They hoped and believed instead that political deals like the Missouri Compromise could satisfy both sides.

Imagine waking up on the day of the test and being startled to realize you were unprepared. It must have been terrifying for people as they each reached their day of dawning, finally realizing that no deals could make things all right again and that war was around the corner. They would have to acknowledge that bloodshed had already occurred in places like Kansas (as Kansas, Missouri, and other midwestern areas were painfully aware). And they have to have known violence was coming closer. They were past the point of no return.

The innocent and the not-so-innocent stood side-by-side in the doorway of one of the most painful chapters in American history. The deep disagreements of how to define and apply the principles of freedom and liberty tore the country apart, tore states apart, and tore families apart. Life as they knew it was over, and things would never be the same again.

By showing the original and modern language of important documents and speeches side-by-side in this book, we hoped to make this segment of our nation's history more understandable for everyone. Nineteenth-century language was formal and not much like the way we talk today. But the meaning behind the words is critically important, as everyone, not just politicians and military leaders, tried to work out what the nation stood for.

What this book tried to show is how everyday people, people like you and me, were affected by the political actions and angry whirlwinds that picked them up and deposited them into a tornado of war and destruction. With our new understanding of that history, we may see a reflection of today's daily media bombardment telling us about the deep disagreements plaguing our country. The lessons of our history may, just may, help us to wake up in time to study for the test, to recognize the direction in which we are headed, and to do what we can to change the course before we pass the point of no return. How do we do this? By not overlooking injustice. By respecting our fellow citizens, no matter who they are. By electing leaders whose goals are for the good of the country.

Let us recall the clarity the Civil War leaders had about their beliefs and follow in their footsteps by truly understanding what we think and what we want for the future and not just jump on a bandwagon because others have. If Lincoln and Davis, Lee and Grant, and many more could respectfully disagree, so can we. When more of us understand our past, we can be better prepared to shape the future.

Bonus Chapter 1: Comparing the United States Constitution and the Confederate Constitution

The US Constitution was written in 1787, and the Confederate Constitution was written in 1861. In those 74 years, thoughts and practices have changed for many people. Therefore, this comparison only shows how people were feeling in 1861.

Title	UNITED STATES OF AMERICA	CONFEDERATE STATES OF AMERICA
Preamble	We the People of the United States, in Order to form a more perfect Union… (Emphasizes Union)	We, the people of the Confederate States, each State acting in its sovereign and independent character… (Emphasizes states' rights)
Slavery	Does not mention slavery but uses terms like "other persons." Allows Congress to ban slavery.	Uses the word slavery and guarantees protection of the practice. Forbids the Congress from banning slavery throughout the Confederacy and forbids individual states from banning slavery.
Slave Trade	Allowed Congress to ban the international slave trade (and it did so in 1808).	Banned the international slave trade but allowed interstate slave trade.
Territories	Congress was given broad authority over US territories.	Required slavery to be recognized in all CSA territories.
Executive Term Limits	The President's term in office was set to 4	Presidents were limited to one 6-year term.

	years with no limit on the number of terms. (A 2-term limit was added through the 22nd Amendment in 1951.)	
Line-Item Veto	Presidents may reject entire bills sent forward by Congress but may not pick and choose what they like and do not like from the bill.	Presidents may cancel selected portions of bills such as denying funding for a specific item or program.
Protective Tariffs	Tariffs may be imposed by Congress but not by the President without Congressional consent for the purpose of promoting U.S. industry.	Congress is forbidden from using tariffs or taxes to help industry.
Cabinet Members in Congress	Cabinet members may not sit in Congress.	Cabinet members may participate in debates but not vote in either house of Congress.
Amendments	An amendment may pass only with the support of two thirds of both Houses of Congress and three quarters of the states.	This was the same but with more emphasis on the independence of each state.
Supremacy Clause	"This Constitution shall be the supreme law of the land."	This was included but with emphasis on the independence of each state.
New States	Congress may admit new states.	New states could be admitted but slavery had to be recognized if the state was south of the Mason-Dixon line.

Revenue Bills	Must originate in Congress in the House of Representatives.	This was the same, but every spending bill had to contain the specific amount and purpose. No general or "catch-all" spending bills were permitted.
General Tone	Focused on creating a strong but balanced federal government.	Aimed at creating a looser federation of states while protecting the slavery practice.

Bonus Chapter 2: Major Battles of the Civil War

Title	**The Battle of Fort Sumter**
Where	Charleston Harbor, South Carolina
When	April 12, 1861
How Many Died	2 casualties were caused by a misfire during a 100-gun salute.
Who Won	Confederacy
Important Facts	This was the battle that kicked off the Civil War. Confederate troops attacked Fort Sumter shortly after Abraham Lincoln's inauguration as President on March 4, 1861.

Title	**The First Battle of Bull Run**
Where	Manassas, Virginia
When	July 17-21, 1861
How Many Died	Confederate: 387; Union: 460
Who Won	Confederacy
Important Facts	This was the first full-scale battle of the Civil War, fought just 25 miles from Washington DC. Lincoln was under pressure from the public to end the rebellion in 90 days, so he sent 35,000 poorly trained troops under General Irvin McDowell to capture Richmond, the Confederal capital. They were stopped on their way by Confederate General P.G.T. Beauregard's 32,000 troops, who were also very green. The Confederate line was reinforced when Beauregard was joined by General Joseph Johnston and General Thomas Jackson (later known as "Stonewall" Jackson) and their troops. This is when many on both sides began to realize the war was not going to be quick or easy.

Title	**The Battle of Wilson's Creek**
Where	Springfield, Missouri
When	August 10, 1861

How Many Died	Confederate: 277; Union: 258
Who Won	Confederacy
Important Facts	This was the first major battle to be fought west of the Mississippi. Missouri was a border state where feelings were divided about slavery. Many supported the Union and many supported the Confederacy. Union Brigadier General Nathanial Lyon launched a surprise attack on a Confederate camp of 11,000 with 5,400 troops. He was killed in action. While Confederate troops won the battle through sheer numbers, the Confederacy never gained control of Missouri.

Title	The Battle of Ball's Bluff
Where	Leesburg, Virginia
When	October 21, 1861
How Many Died	Confederate: 36; Union: 223
Who Won	Confederacy
Important Facts	The Union decided to try to secure Northern Virginia and relied on incorrect information that said the Confederates were not well defended. Union scouts also mistook trees for a Confederate camp. This significantly hampered the assault. Union commander Colonel Edward Baker, who was also a sitting Senator, was killed, making him the only member of Congress to die in combat. Some of the Union deaths were due to drowning as they tried to retreat back across the Potomac River toward Washington. Ball's Bluff was a crushing defeat for the Union and a major boost to Confederate morale. After this, the Union proceeded much more cautiously and with better training.

Title	The Battle of Shiloh
Where	Southwestern Tennessee near Pittsburg Landing
When	April 6-7, 1862
How Many Died	Confederate: 1,728; Union: 1,754
Who Won	Union
Important Facts	This battle came at a terrible cost to both sides. Confederate General Johnston, considered the South's best, was killed. Union General Ulysses Grant was criticized for not being well prepared and for the high loss of life. After the battle there were calls to remove him, but Lincoln defended him as a general who fights. For some, his steady leadership under pressure improved his reputation. This victory in Tennessee opened the way for Union troops to advance West and South.

Title	The Battle of Antietam
Where	Sharpsburg, Maryland
When	September 17, 1862
How Many Died	Confederate: 1,546; Union: 2,108
Who Won	It was close but considered a Union victory by driving Lee to retreat to Virginia.
Important Facts	This battle marked Confederate General Robert E. Lee's first invasion of the North. A major Union advantage came when Lee's battle plans went missing and were found by a Union soldier, wrapped around cigars. Union General George McClellan fumbled that advantage by delaying too long, which allowed Confederate troops to better organize. McClellan was later removed from command for his indecisiveness.

Title	The Battle and Siege of Vicksburg
Where	Vicksburg, Mississippi
When	May 18 to July 4, 1863 (47 days)

How Many Died	Confederate: 3.202; Union: 3,940
Who Won	Union
Important Facts	Vicksburg was considered to be the "Gibraltar of the Confederacy" due to its strategic position controlling Mississippi River traffic. Lincoln said, "Vicksburg is the key. The war can never be brought to a close until that key is in our pocket." General Ulysses Grant won in a series of battles around the Vicksburg area, literally surrounding it and stopping Confederate reinforcements. He then bombarded Vicksburg with incessant shelling and cut off supplies. Citizens moved to caves to escape the shelling. On July 4th, Confederate General John Pemberton surrendered a starving, exhausted, and demoralized army and city. Union control of Vicksburg split the Confederacy, cutting off Texas, Louisiana, and Arkansas from the rest of the South. The memory of this difficult time scarred the city, which did not celebrate the 4th of July until after World War II.

Title	The Battle of Gettysburg
Where	Gettysburg, Pennsylvania
When	July 1-3, 1863
How Many Died	Confederate: 3,903; Union: 3,155
Who Won	Union
Important Facts	Confederate General Robert E. Lee attacked Union troops on July 1, hoping to continue to push North toward peace negotiations. Union General John Buford established a strong defensive position on high ground as heavy fighting continued for two more days. A series of smaller but fierce battles took place around the area but Union forces stayed in the key positions. The Confederate hope of turning the tide with Pickett's Charge (General George Pickett) where 15,000 troops charged across open fields

	toward the Union line. This resulted in heavy Confederate losses and the loss of the overall battle. With a total of 51,000 casualties, The Battle of Gettysburg was the bloodiest battle of the Civil War.

Title	Sherman's March to the Sea
Where	Atlanta, Georgia to Savannah, Georgia (285 miles)
When	November 15 to December 21, 1864
How Many Died	Confederate: ~1,000 to 2,000; Union: ~1,500
Who Won	Union
Important Facts	Union General William Tecumseh Sherman captured Atlanta, destroying military facilities, industry, and civilian necessities such as railroads. His aim was to shorten the war by crippling the Confederacy, but his plan was extremely controversial. Sherman's troops destroyed factories, farms, and supplies, seized livestock, and burned crops. Throughout the march of destruction, there were no large battles but a long, spread-out source of fear and panic. Thousands of people were displaced and millions of dollars in property was destroyed. After demolishing Georgia's ability to wage war, Sherman marched north through the Carolinas, continuing his scorched-earth path. This devastation led directly to the collapse of the Confederacy in 1865.

Title	The Fall of Richmond
Where	Richmond, Virginia – capital of the Confederacy
When	April 2-3, 1865
How Many Died	Casualties were relatively small but thousands of citizens were displaced
Who Won	Union
Important Facts	The psychological toll of the capital's fall was as crushing as the physical toll. Supply lines were cut

off and Lee's army was greatly weakened by desertions. General Lee wired Jefferson Davis, the President of the Confederacy, that he could not hold Richmond. Richmond was evacuated and Confederate forces destroyed warehouses and supplies so they would not be captured by Union troops. On April 3, Union soldiers, including regiments made up of former slaves, raised the Union flag over the city. President Abraham Lincoln toured Richmond on April 4.

Title	The Battle of Appomattox Courthouse
Where	Appomattox Courthouse, Virginia
When	April 9, 1865
How Many Died	Confederate: 500 (killed and wounded); Union: 164
Who Won	Union
Important Facts	This battle ended the war in Virginia. Union General Ulysses Grant had superior numbers of troops and great morale behind him following previous Union victories at Shiloh, Vicksburg, and Gettysburg. Confederate General Robert E. Lee's troops were surrounded and had no escape routes. He met with Grant at the home of Wilmer McLean to discuss surrender terms. Grant generously allowed Confederate soldiers to keep their horses and personal weapons provided they pledged not to fight again.

It would be reasonable to think that the surrender at Appomattox Courthouse was the end of the Civil War. However, in the 1860's news travelled slowly. Also, some commanders refused to give up. Several battles occurred after the surrender including the Battle of Fort Blakely (Mobile, Alabama), the Battle of Columbus (Columbus, Georgia), the Battle of Palmito Ranch (Brownsville, Texas), and the Skirmish at Hobdy's Bridge (Eufaula, Alabama). All were Union victories except the Battle of Palmito Ranch, which was won by Confederate troops. But, despite this victory, they surrendered a few weeks later after news of Appomattox reached the area.

Bonus Chapter 3: Timeline of Major Events in the U.S. Civil War (1860–1865)

1860

Nov 6 — Abraham Lincoln elected President (without carrying a single Southern state).

Dec 20 — South Carolina secedes from the Union (first state to do so).

1861

Jan–Feb — Six more states secede (Mississippi, Florida, Alabama, Georgia, Louisiana, Texas).

Feb 9 — Confederate States of America formed, Jefferson Davis elected President.

Mar 4 — Lincoln's First Inaugural Address: pledges to preserve the Union, says he has no intention to abolish slavery where it already exists.

Apr 12–14 — Battle of Fort Sumter: Confederates fire the first shots of the Civil War; Union surrenders the fort.

Apr–May — Four more states secede (Virginia, Arkansas, Tennessee, North Carolina).

Jul 21 — First Battle of Bull Run (Manassas): first major land battle; Confederate victory shocks the North.

1862

Feb — Union victories at **Fort Henry and Fort Donelson** (Tennessee).

Apr 6–7 — Battle of Shiloh (Tennessee).

Sep 17 — Battle of Antietam (Maryland): bloodiest single day in U.S. history.

Sep 22 — Preliminary Emancipation Proclamation issued.

1863

Jan 1 — **Emancipation Proclamation** takes effect.

May 18 – Jul 4 — **Siege of Vicksburg** (Mississippi).

Jul 1–3 — **Battle of Gettysburg** (Pennsylvania).

Nov 19 — **Gettysburg Address** delivered by Lincoln.

1864

May–Sep — **Grant's Overland Campaign** and **Sherman's Atlanta Campaign**.

Sep 2 — **Fall of Atlanta**.

Nov 8 — **Lincoln reelected President**, defeating George B. McClellan.

Nov 15 – Dec 21 — **Sherman's March to the Sea**.

1865

Mar 4 — **Lincoln's Second Inaugural Address**: calls for healing "with malice toward none, with charity for all."

Apr 2 — **Fall of Richmond**, Confederate capital captured.

Apr 9 — **Surrender at Appomattox Court House**: General Lee surrenders to General Grant.

Apr 14 — **Lincoln assassinated** at Ford's Theatre by John Wilkes Booth.

Apr 26 — Confederate General Johnston surrenders in North Carolina.

Dec 6 — **13th Amendment ratified**, officially abolishing slavery in the United States.